The Truth About Elderly Narcissists

By Cynthia Bailey–Rug

Other books by this author:

Non-fiction:

It's Not You, It's Them: When People are More Than Selfish
Children And Narcissistic Personality Disorder: A Guide For Parents
Life After Narcissistic Abuse: There Is Healing And Hope
It's All About Me! The Facts About Maternal Narcissism
You Are Not Alone!
Emerging From The Chrysalis
A Witness Of Faith
Lessons From The Heart: What Animals Have Taught Me About Life And Love
All I Know About Marriage...I Learned The Hard Way!
Pawprints On Our Hearts
Baptism Of Joy
Romantic Inspirations
Facets Of Love

Fiction:

Sins Of The Father
The Christian Woman's Guide To Killing Her Husband

Table Of Contents

Introduction

Fewer things in life are more challenging and painful than having a narcissistic parent. One of those few things is having an elderly narcissistic parent or relative that you are expected to care for in their golden years. The goal of this book is to help you to cope with this extremely difficult situation.

I first learned about the challenges of caring for an elderly narcissist in 2000. My narcissistic maternal grandmother's husband had a stroke, and she put him in a nursing home. She was too frail to care for herself, let alone him as well, so sadly, this was his best option. Unfortunately for me, this put me in the position of becoming her main caregiver for a year, since I lived closer to her than any other relatives. Although I knew nothing of Narcissistic Personality Disorder at that time, I knew something was very wrong with her and the way she treated people. She was vicious and verbally abusive to some of us who were closest to her, and pleasant to strangers, acquaintances and her doctors. I prayed often during that time, and God showed me ways to cope with her awful behavior. I could not have survived that awful time without God's help.

At the time of writing this book, my parents are in their late seventies. My mother, the overt narcissist, is in rather good health. She has some minor problems including having back problems, which is why she says she cannot do much housework, no laundry, carrying groceries, etc. My father, once the covert narcissist but becoming more overt, has many serious health problems including Alzheimer's, seizures stemming from a traumatic brain injury, carotid artery disease, strokes, stage three kidney disease and more. There have been times I have helped my parents, although I never have been their full time caregiver.

Also, because of writing about narcissistic abuse, many of my readers have shared their experiences with their narcissistic parents with me. As a result of their experiences and mine, I have learned a lot about dealing with elderly narcissists. I am not a mental health professional, but I have gained a great deal of knowledge about narcissists and narcissistic abuse thanks to my experiences and those of the people who have shared their stories with me. I pray this knowledge will help you in your situation!

I also have found my relationship with God to be absolutely vital in my life, especially when it comes to the subject of narcissists. In this book, I mention prayer or my faith often. If you do not share my faith, I hope you will continue reading anyway, as I believe this book still can help you. Please though, keep an open mind. God is so good and loving, and He truly wants to help you in every area of your life. Please consider giving Him a chance if you have not done so before.

For the sake of simplicity, I will refer to the elderly narcissists in this book as female and as a parent where appropriate. However, the information is also applicable to male narcissists or those in roles other than being a parent.

Chapter One – Some About Aging Narcissists

Most people who are aware of the existence of Narcissistic Personality Disorder know the basic signs that all narcissists share to varying degrees:

- Lack of empathy.
- Extreme sense of entitlement.
- Very insecure yet constantly tries to hide it.
- Giving the impression of believing that they are very special or unique in some way or both.
- Constantly in search of narcissistic supply (anything to boost the narcissist's fragile self esteem).
- Overly sensitive to criticism, and will rage if they receive it. Narcissistic rage also may happen if supply is denied. A rage may include screaming or getting physically violent. Others give the silent treatment,

refusing to speak to or acknowledge the critical person until an apology is given to the narcissist.

- Brags about their accomplishments, complements and praise received. Their insecurity leads them to do this to convince others as well as themselves that they are as special, talented, beautiful, etc. as they say they are.
- Extremely manipulative.
- Extremely controlling.
- Extremely envious. Narcissists simply cannot stand to see other people happy or enjoying something. They will either openly tear down whatever the person is enjoying, or do it in a more subtle manner ("I suppose that's nice if you like that sort of thing", refusing to acknowledge or speak about it, etc.)
- Actively enjoys causing pain in others or is completely oblivious to the pain they cause due to being completely self – absorbed.
- They have double standards (the "do as I say, not as I do" mindset).
- Actively project their flaws onto others. In other words, if the narcissist is a liar, they accuse other people of lying constantly. If unfaithful to their spouse, the spouse is accused of cheating.
- Must be the center of attention at all times.
- They do not possess any healthy coping skills whatsoever.

- They have selective memory. In other words, they will forget things that make them look bad. They also may twist that situation around when discussing it so they either look good or look like the victim.
- Can turn any conversation back to themselves.

Narcissistic Personality Disorder is also what is known as a spectrum disorder. Some folks with it who fall lower on the spectrum only show some of the symptoms. They often can be dealt with fairly easily and successfully. Others who are high on the spectrum, malignant narcissists, are much harder and often impossible to deal with. These people are the ones who show many or even all of the symptoms.

Did you realize that there are also two types of narcissists? There are overt and covert narcissists.

Overt narcissists are the type that is impossible to ignore. There is a lot more information on overt narcissists readily available. They are bold in their abusive actions, and abrasive in their personality. They often have loud voices that carry. When they are angry, look out! The overt narcissist often screams, rants and raves, and sometimes they become physically abusive. They are the easy narcissists to spot, simply because of being so obvious in their behavior.

Covert narcissists are the opposite. They are much quieter, and often come across very giving and unselfish, even martyr like. They are not giving out of the goodness of their hearts, however. They only give to make others think they are good people. Covert narcissists still hurt people just as much as overt narcissists, but they always twist things around to make it look like they were trying to do someone a favor, they simply did not know any better or they are the "real victim" in the situation.

Quite often, if you realize one person is a narcissist, that person's spouse will be one too. Overt and covert narcissists often marry, and it is a perfect, dysfunctional match. The overt loves being in the limelight, and the covert is perfectly content being in the background. The covert narcissist enjoys when the overt narcissist acts out and others see the awful behavior, because the covert then will be viewed as the kind, long suffering spouse. Also, the overt narcissist's outlandish behavior attracts so much attention, the covert's quieter abusive actions attracts little to no attention. The covert narcissist may abuse without limits because everyone's attention is on the overt. Covert narcissists also portray themselves in such a way that people rarely confront them, because they think this person simply does not know any better. Or, they are not confronted because they act like a victim, leaving the real victim confused and feeling guilty for saying anything at all.

My parents are a prime example of this scenario. My mother has always been the overt narcissist, my father the covert. She would scream at me, belittle me, and control my every move as a child. My father would not do such things, but he also did nothing to protect me from her abuse. He claimed he had no power to intervene because when I was very young, my mother once told him that she would handle disciplining me, and he needed to stay out of it. If I told my father of something awful my mother did to me, he often would tell me it was hard for him not to be able to help me, and I would end up comforting him.

The few people that knew about my home life thought my father was a good father and a good man, and my mother was the only abusive parent. The truth of the matter though is that both of my parents were extremely abusive, just in very different ways. It is obvious what my mother did to me was wrong, but my father failing to protect me was equally wrong. And, for him to expect me to put up with the abuse as well as comfort him when I was suffering was simply inexcusable. Both of my parents' actions told me that I was unimportant, that I did not matter in the slightest to them, and I was only supposed to do for and care about them.

As narcissists age, their narcissistic actions change along with their bodies. Often covert narcissists turn into more overt ones, no longer hiding behind the martyr mask. They do not even try to look innocent any longer, and they obviously enjoy the pain and troubles they inflict on those around them. They may bark out orders rather than use guilt and manipulation to get their way. Overt narcissists may no longer hit, scream, rant and rage, but they are just as abusive as ever. Their actions often become much more controlled and subtle.

I cannot say with absolute certainty why narcissists often change their actions so drastically, but I have a couple of ideas.

Aging takes away so much. You can lose your looks, your sharp mind, and your friends and family who pass away before you do. Maybe narcissists become angry about these natural events, and because of that anger, no longer have the patience or whatever they need to hide their abusive ways like they once did.

Also, as people age and become frailer, they can no longer be physically intimidating as they once were. They have to get creative if they want to continue intimidating and abusing people.

Or, maybe some think because they are old, they have the right to do whatever they want. No doubt you have heard some elderly person claim that because they are now of a certain age, they can do and say anything they like. These people falsely believe that age gives a free pass to be a jerk. They fail to realize that barring situations such as brain injury or disease which removes one's ability to understand right from wrong, there is no excuse to be a jerk.

Sometimes there are physical causes for a narcissist changing their behavior. Some types of dementia where people lose all memories can actually improve the behavior of narcissists. They may cause a patient to calm down, and eventually stop speaking and doing many activities, including abusive ones. Or, there is Alzheimer's which can make the narcissist act even worse for a while. The typical

Alzheimer's patient loses more short term memory than long term for quite some time during the disease. This means they can remember how they always have acted and felt, so now they act and feel the same ways but with the added challenges, frustration and anger of dealing with Alzheimer's on top of it.

Many narcissists, with or without dementia or brain problems, become much more entitled as they age. I was one of the family caregivers for my narcissistic grandmother for about one year before she stopped speaking to me (I still have no idea why she did that, but I digress...). All of my life, she had been very difficult and mean spirited. Once she needed her family to help take care of her though, she became excessively entitled. I lived about one mile from her at the time, so she called me more than anyone else when she needed help. She just assumed I would ask how high when she said I should jump. Time of day or night did not matter, and neither did anything I needed to do for myself or my family. Her actions told me she thought she was all that should matter in my world. Not knowing about Narcissistic Personality Disorder at the time, I did whatever she wanted, as much as I hated it. In talking to others who have dealt with elderly narcissists, my grandmother seems to be very typical in this way. They seem to think being old and needing help means the people in their lives must cater to their every whim and do for them without any thought to their own health or life.

When you see your narcissistic parent getting worse or even developing more awful behaviors, it may be very hard or even impossible for you to feel pity for your narcissistic parent's struggles and indignities. You may look at someone who suffers in the same way as your parent and feel great pity for them, yet absolutely nothing for your parent. I felt this way concerning my narcissistic grandmother. She was very frail, and I felt no pity for her. Yet, I felt a great deal of pity for other people who were in a similar physical state to hers. Although this can be a great source of guilt and wondering what is wrong with you, rest assured, you are normal. How can you feel "warm and fuzzy" towards someone who always has been and continues to be abusive and cruel? Galatians 6:7 says, *"Be not deceived; God is not mocked: for whatsoever a man soweth, that shall he also reap."* Your narcissistic parent has sown some very bad seeds with you by abusing you. They simply cannot reap a harvest of love and kindness after abusing someone for their lifetime. Try not to beat yourself up for your feelings. They are very natural and understandable under the circumstances.

Chapter Two – Protecting Yourself From Elderly Narcissists

As I mentioned previously, age does not mean that narcissists soften up. Their tactics may change, but they usually are just as cruel if not crueler than they were in their younger days.

When I was growing up, especially in my later teen years, my mother would scream and rage at me on a constant basis. She would tell me what a horrible person I was, and how people were talking about me behind my back because I was so horrible. Sometimes she would question me, interrogate me really, and accuse me of outrageous things I was not doing. It got bad enough that I would admit to doing things I was not doing just to end the interrogation. (A bit of trivia: some cults have been known to do this when a cult member is suspected of disobeying their laws, and the person being interrogated often did the same as I did – admitted to things they did not do in order to end the interrogation.) She even attacked me physically a couple of times. Now that she is in her late seventies, she is not so strong anymore, so her tactics had to change if she wanted to continue abusing me, which she certainly wanted to do. One of her favorite things to do at this stage in her life is quietly to say the cruelest and most hurtful things she can to me say in a very calm demeanor when we are in a public place such as a restaurant. I could not understand why she did that, so several years ago, I asked God about it after a particularly difficult visit with my parents. He gave me my answer. She tries to goad me into getting so angry that I cannot take it anymore and start yelling at her. This would work well for her. People around us would obviously be disgusted with me yelling at my "poor elderly mother for no reason" or something along those lines. Maybe someone would even intervene or call the police on me if I was angry enough. Thank God for showing me what her goal was, so I have learned not to raise my voice to her when she has done this. I stay calm in her presence, then vent later to my husband or a friend when I am away from her.

Many people say narcissists never change but they do. They adapt to their aging bodies and minds by changing the ways in which they abuse their victims. If you are going to deal with them, you must learn new ways to adapt to their new behaviors.

There are ways to do this! You can keep your sanity if you continue to stay in a relationship with your narcissistic parent. It will not be easy sometimes, but it is possible.

The main thing I can recommend is to pray. Ask God to provide you with anything you need to be able to handle the relationship with your parent in healthy, mature ways – wisdom, insight, strength, courage or anything else you can think of. If you cannot think of anything, then simply ask Him to give you whatever He knows you need. I also have asked for creative ways to cope, and God has provided them time and time again.

I also highly recommend praying for your narcissistic parent. I know how truly hard this can be! After they have hurt and used you so much, it is easy to get to the point of not caring about them at all. I get that. I often feel the same way, but, in spite of that, I pray for my parents daily. In fact, I set a reminder on my cell phone to remind me to pray every morning so I do not forget. It also helps to motivate me a bit if I do not want to pray for them, because I know God and I have a scheduled "date" every day at that time.

Matthew 5:44 says, *"But I say unto you, Love your enemies, bless them that curse you, do good to them that hate you, and pray for them which despitefully use you, and persecute you;",* so praying for your narcissistic parents is obviously something God wants you to do. It would not be in the Bible otherwise.

Praying for our enemies opens doors for them to see the error of their ways and make changes, to be blessed, and also possibly to come to the knowledge of the love of God. No matter how you feel about your parents at the moment, how hurt and angry you may be (and your feelings are very valid!), I hope you would wish them to have such things.

It also opens the doors for blessings to come your way as well. Jeremiah 29:7 states, *"And seek the peace of the city whither I have caused you to be carried away captives, and pray unto the Lord for it: for in the peace thereof shall ye have peace."* In the New International Version translation it says, *"Also, seek the peace and prosperity of the city to which I have carried you into exile. Pray to the Lord for it, because if it prospers, you too will prosper." (NIV)* Praying for others, especially your enemies, can open the door for great blessings to come your way.

Since I have begun praying daily for my parents as well as others who have hurt, mistreated or even abused me, I have noticed I have more peace than I once did too. I cannot find a Scripture to back that up, unfortunately, but I can tell you it is the truth in my experience.

Journaling can be very helpful as well. I use an online, password protected, private journal to be absolutely certain it never falls into the wrong hands. Journaling helps you by providing you with a safe place to get all of your feelings and concerns out without any fear of judgment. Writing also can help you to have clarity that speaking does not provide. There is something about seeing things written down or typed out on your computer screen that helps make things clearer and easier to understand. Seeing things in writing also helps to validate you somehow. Writing my autobiography in 2012 really helped me to see just how many horrible experiences I have survive in my life.

Always appear calm and peaceful in the presence of a narcissist no matter what. They get narcissistic supply by feeling powerful if they can upset you. Do not provide that narcissistic supply by reacting out of hurt, anger or frustration! I learned a very useful technique that can help you to do this. It is a way for those who care for Alzheimer's patients to cope when they get frustrated, but it works well in many circumstances, I believe. Many of my readers and I have experienced a great deal of success with this technique. Inhale deeply then exhale. This will help to calm you down physically and give you a moment to consider your response before speaking.

Sometimes as narcissistic parents get older and meaner, their adult children end up racked with guilt. They get so frustrated with their parent's high expectations of them and tired of the years of narcissistic abuse, that they want their parent to die. Many will not admit this out loud, but they feel it anyway. Although it is a very normal way to feel, even knowing that can make a person feel terribly guilty. If you feel this way too, please do not beat yourself up for it! Under the circumstances, it is quite normal. Instead, accept your feelings without judgment. Know that you are not a bad person for feeling this way, and that feeling it does not mean you would act on it by hurting your parent. It might help you to write it out in your journal, too.

One thing I have found oddly beneficial is accepting my narcissistic parents as they are. I do not mean tolerating their abuse at all, so please do not think accepting them equals allowing them to be abusive! That is not the case at all! What I do mean is accepting the facts that they are narcissists, abusive, and probably never will change unless it is to get worse. Accepting those facts helped me to release expectations with my parents. I know beyond a doubt that this time I communicate with them is not going to be better. This time is going to be just as bad as last time and the time before, or possibly even worse. I also accept the fact that they do not want to change, so they will not change, unless a miracle happens and they suddenly decide they want to change. This helps you to have realistic expectations with your parent, which means you will not be disappointed every time you must deal with her.

Accepting your parent also means you accept that they have a problem, Narcissistic Personality Disorder. The benefit of accepting that fact means that you are not the problem, they are! Contrary to what they always have said or implied, they are the problem, not you. Accepting that truth that they are the real problem can be a huge challenge for many adult children of narcissistic parents, since they blame their children for everything, but it needs to be done for the sake of your mental health.

Closely related to accepting your narcissistic parent, I have found a degree of understanding them can help as well. I realize many people disagree with me on this topic. They think understanding your parent can make you willing to tolerate her abusive ways by making you pity them. Or, they think it is a lack of maturity or intelligence to try to understand abusive people. I disagree with these mindsets however, and I will tell you why.

If you can understand why your parents do the things they do, it can help you immensely. When you understand that they are only doing things to gain narcissistic supply or to exercise control over you, it helps you to avoid falling for their manipulations. When you understand the scathing criticisms are to hurt you in order to build themselves up, the criticisms hurt less. In fact, the thing that your parent criticizes so harshly is most likely a point of envy. She envies your talent, your success or even your looks so much that she wants to try to take that away from you. Realizing that fact makes the criticisms hurt less, because they become less of a personal attack and more about what they truly are – your narcissistic parent's insecurities. When your narcissistic parent tries to hurt you with vicious, scathing criticisms, remembering what the criticisms are really about can help you to maintain a calm demeanor.

Using logic can help with the scathing criticisms, too. For example, let's say you slip up a bit. Instead of taking that deep breath and responding calmly to your narcissistic mother's criticisms, you react out of your hurt and anger by yelling at her. In return, your mother criticizes you for being upset. When this happens (and it will happen — we all slip sometimes!), say something like, "Yes, Mom, you're absolutely right. Why would I be upset that you said that snarky comment about ___? Nobody else in the whole wide world would be upset when something (or someone) they love is criticized. I just don't know what's wrong with me! I'm sooooooo crazy! You're absolutely right!" then roll your eyes. Narcissists usually do not know what to say or do with comments like that. It shows the ridiculousness of their words and actions, so how can they turn things around so their words or actions look good? They simply cannot at this point! They are stumped! At this point they may give the silent treatment, change the subject or laugh things off as if nothing happened.

You also need to remember that you have power now. Your parent is not in control of you any longer. You are an adult now, not a helpless child at the mercy of a narcissistic parent. You do not deserve to be treated as a child. Narcissistic parents love treating their grown child as if he or she is still a young child. This is because of the narcissistic parent's deep need to control their child. My mother does this (well, she does when she is not giving me the silent treatment, that is) and I find it infuriating! She talks about things I did as a child as if they happened yesterday. And, the things are not good things, like when I graduated in the top ten percent of my high school class, made honor roll constantly or other accomplishments. Instead she likes to bring up stupid or embarrassing things I did as a child, or times she claims she "rescued" me in some way. She also seems to think my tastes have not changed since I was around fifteen years old, fails to realize many things I once liked, I no longer enjoy and that I have

15

developed new interests. She also likes to boss me around, and she expects me to accept it and blindly obey.

To deal with this infuriating behavior, I started by asking God for some creativity. Simply saying, "That is embarrassing (or hurtful, etc) so please do not talk about it" never works with narcissists. If they know something bothers you, they will not only continue to do the behavior, but do it even more, then criticize you for getting upset. This is exactly why I asked God for creative ways to deal with her nastiness, to avoid that painful scenario.

I ended up getting somewhat sarcastic with my mother. When she told stories, I would make snide comments like, "Oh yea. Never heard this one before." "That's a story worth sharing for the hundredth time." While that might let her know it bothered me, it also gave her a slight narcissistic injury by showing my disdain for something she was talking about. It was not enough of a narcissistic injury for her to rage about, but it was enough to get her attention. She would laugh it off and change the subject.

When she would comment about things I liked as a child yet no longer like, I simply reminded her that I am no longer fifteen (or ten or however old I was when I liked that thing she mentioned). Again, it caused a slight narcissistic injury that caused her to stop in her tracks.

When my mother bossed me around, it never used to bother me. That was just how she was and I never thought too much about it. Then one day a couple of years ago, in my own home, my mother told me to get her something. I blindly obeyed. She smiled a smug little grin at me when I handed her the item, and something inside me snapped. I realized she was getting a narcissistic thrill from my obedience! I inadvertently provided her with narcissistic supply! That is when I realized this had to stop. I am not the hired help, I am her daughter, and to top it off, it was my home! No one orders me around in my own home! So immediately I asked God to show me how to deal with it, and He did. I cannot recall if it was in the same visit or a later one, but again, my mother bossed me around in my own home. I got the item she wanted, and as I handed it to her I said, "Since you asked me so nicely of course I got it for you. You're very welcome!" I smiled brightly as I handed her the item. She was stunned and muttered a quiet, "thank you" under her breath. Several days later, my mother called to ask me to look something up online for her (my parents do not have a computer), and she politely asked me to look something up for her if I had a minute. I loved it! For once, she did not treat me like her employee and showed me some basic respect! This was a major victory for me!

In the couple of years that passed since I first put an end to my mother's bossing me around, she has slipped up a few times. But, it just takes me smiling and saying something about how nicely she asked me to do that for her to set her back on the right path for a while.

If I can have success in these areas, you certainly can too! Maybe what worked for me will work for you as well. Hopefully it will, but if it does not, then I recommend asking God for help in this area. You certainly do NOT need to be treated like a child when you are an adult! It is disrespectful to you and your parent does not deserve to control you.

Another helpful thing I learned to do when dealing with my narcissistic parents is to become incredibly boring to them. Some call this the Gray Rock Method. By this I mean that I provide little to no narcissistic supply, I answer their questions as succinctly as possible, share virtually no information about my life, show no emotion around them and pretend not to notice their attempts at guilt or control..

First, do not offer them praise, which means they get no narcissistic supply. If something praiseworthy comes up, complements are kept to an absolute minimum. "That's nice." "Good." They do not need to see any emotions you may be feeling either. Stay a blank slate, even in the midst of very good news.

Second, by answering questions succinctly, this provides them only the information they need to know, nothing else that could get twisted around or used to cause pain some way at a future date. Yes and no and other one word answers can be your best friend.

Third, sharing no information about your life with a narcissistic parent means they have nothing new to criticize about you. It makes life much simpler by eliminating "insult ammunition". If my parents ask how I am, I say I am fine. What have I been doing lately? Not much. How is So and So? She is fine. Short, vague answers eliminate insult ammunition, and the narcissist cannot say anything to show their anger about you behaving this way without looking bad. This means they will not say anything, as much as they may want to, since narcissists avoid looking bad at all costs. It actually can be rather amusing watching how angry they get knowing they cannot say anything to you for ruining their "fun."

Fourth, showing narcissists no emotion is always a wise move. If they realize they can stir up strong emotions in you (preferably anger or tears), this gives them a tremendous amount of narcissistic supply. It makes them feel powerful for having such control over a person. I hold my feelings in until I am away from my parents' presence, and can vent my feelings safely. (I think this is the only benefit of learning early on never to show emotion around narcissistic parents — as an adult, you have the ability to hide your feelings until it is safe to let them out.)

Lastly, it is also important not to fall for their manipulations or attempts to control. Ignore them when possible, pretending not to notice anything.

Becoming boring in these ways makes narcissists lose interest in you very quickly once they realize they no longer can get what they want from you.

Also important in protecting yourself from your narcissistic parents is to focus on your healing. It is always important to focus on your healing, but perhaps even more so when you are still in a relationship with your narcissistic parents. This is very important for two reasons. One, you will get healthier and stronger, which naturally benefits you greatly. Two, getting healthier and stronger means your narcissistic parents can hurt and control you less. And, as an added bonus, the healthier you are, the less any narcissist will want to do with you because you are much harder for them to manipulate, control and hurt. I have seen this work with my parents. The healthier I have gotten, the less they have wanted to do with me. They used to call me several times a week, but as I got healthier, their calls dwindled greatly.

Elderly narcissists often like to use the pity card to gain control and attention. They complain about being old, their health problems, and not being able to do things anymore that they once did. While granted these things are certainly not fun and most people complain about them at some point, narcissists use these normal occurrences as a means of control and for attention. My narcissistic grandmother seemed to eat up the attention she got simply for being old. When people periodically would say to her, "How old are you, Darlin'?" she would brag about her age. Then she would grin when they would tell her how well she looked or was doing for her age, and then she would complain about her health problems. Naturally the well—meaning person would say how sorry they were she had these problems, and ask her questions such as what could be done for her. I understand this would be a bit of narcissistic supply for anyone, narcissist or not. Who does not enjoy complements and validation? However, narcissists take it too far. I noticed after this happened with my grandmother, she seemed especially smug and entitled for the rest of the time I was with her. It seemed to me like she thought, "I deserve to be waited on and acknowledged as special because I'm old! That person reminded me of that fact."

You need to be aware of this pity—loving behavior because otherwise your narcissistic parent will use it to the maximum with you. If she can convince you she just does not feel well enough to do the dishes, she will have you coming by daily to do them. And while you are here, could you run the vacuum? You know, those basement steps are so hard on her what with her bad knee and all... why don't you do a load or two of laundry? If you refuse to do such things, your narcissistic parent may pull out another favorite weapon of elderly narcissists — guilt.

All narcissists love guilt, but the elderly ones seem to enjoy it the most. "I understand, you have better things to do than to spend time with me..." "That's OK. I'll just go to the doctor's office all by myself. You don't have to go to the trouble of taking me." Basically if you do not do what they want you to do, you are shamed for being a bad person who does not love your parent. Chances are, your parent will tell others what a bad person you are, how you are never there for your parent, and other nonsense.

Keep in mind what pity—loving and guilt are about with narcissists. They are simply about control and attention. Stay realistic when your narcissistic parent tries to manipulate you with these tools. Should you feel guilty for what you have or have not done? Should you feel sorry for your parent because she cannot do her own laundry, or is the truth that she exaggerating a health problem simply to get you to do it for her? Answer questions honestly and objectively. If you have trouble with objectivity, pretend a good friend of yours is in this situation. Would you tell her she should feel guilty for what she did or did not do? Should she help her parent? Pretending the situation is happening to another person can help you to be much more objective about it. And, it even can help you to think of ways to deal with the situation.

Narcissists, no matter their age, love their flying monkeys. Those evil little minions who are under the delusion that the narcissist is truly a great person as she claims to be, or gets some weird thrill from watching the narcissist hurt their victims. Either way, these people will be more than happy to tell you how horrible you are. How could you hurt your mother like that? Your father just does not know how to show his feelings, but he loves you a great deal, so you should just forgive and forget whatever "you think" he did.

Personally, I believe that unless they truly are naïve enough to fall for the narcissist's "good guy/gal" act, flying monkeys are just as evil as narcissists. They help narcissists abuse their victims — how can that not be evil? They remind me of people who hold down a victim to be raped. Sure, they may not commit the actual rape, but they enabled the rapist to commit the crime. That makes them just as guilty as the rapist, in my opinion.

Elderly narcissists seem to enjoy using flying monkeys and can do so very easily. Maybe it is because no one expects a "little old person" to be anything but sweet. Maybe it is because narcissists are incredibly talented actors, able to convince most people of anything they want to. I do not know for sure, but in any case, if you have elderly narcissistic parents, chances are, you are going to have to deal with flying monkeys at some point.

I find it best to ignore them. Social media makes this especially easy, since you can select what friends see what you post, remove them from your friend's list or you can block people entirely. You also can block people from calling you or sending you text messages or emails. It is a beautiful thing! Unfortunately ignoring flying monkeys is not as easy in real life.

Setting boundaries is a good place to start. At least with some flying monkeys, you have a chance that they will respect those boundaries, unlike narcissists. Simply explain that you do not wish to discuss this topic with them, and if they continue, you will leave the room (or hang up the phone), then follow through with your threat if they continue.

You also can change the subject. If they turn it back to what you do not want to discuss, change it again. Keep doing so if need be. If you get tired of this, end your conversation with them.

Remember, it is important with flying monkeys not to discuss the narcissist or anything personal. They are usually very devoted to the narcissist, so you will not get them to see the truth. Plus, chances are very good they will go back to the narcissist, and tell them whatever you said. You do not want that, as the narcissist will use that information to hurt you somehow.

You may be best off severing ties with the flying monkey, if he or she is especially devoted. Many are so loyal to their narcissist, they will refuse to see or hear any truth, and continually will cause you pain. There is no reaching people like this, sadly. I have experienced this with a couple of people, and it is beyond frustrating. We could not even have simple, pleasant conversations because at some point, something hurtful would be said, ruining the conversation. Maybe because I refused to discuss the topics they wanted to, they quit speaking to me, which is fine with me. I never had to tell them I wanted them out of my life, which made my life a bit easier. I would have done it, however, because it is simply ridiculous when someone cannot respect another person enough to at least try to understand how they feel, or respect them enough to stop discussing a topic when they say they do not wish to discuss a certain matter.

Many elderly narcissists love to use money as a means of control, whether they are rich or poor. Many are on a very limited income, and expect their adult children to pay for whatever they want or need without regard to how their son or daughter is going to pay for it. If this describes your situation, then remember that you have the right to set limits. You do not have to give your parent money every time she asks for it. There are also government programs that could help her, such as food stamps. Check with your local Department of Aging or local churches to guide you to the right places.

If you suspect your narcissistic parent has more money than she lets on, yet continually asks you for money, one way you could find out is to offer to pay a bill for her. If she asks for money to pay her electric bill, for example, then offer to pay it for her. Tell her you need her bill and account number. If she is truly in need, she will provide what you ask for. If she is not, she may insist on you giving her money so she can pay the bill herself or accuse you of not trusting her. Such behaviors can be a clue that she is not truly in need.

If your narcissistic parent has money, it may be held over you. She may threaten to cut you out of her will. Or, she may lend you money when you are in a tight spot, but abuse you more than usual afterwards. Years ago, my husband and I had a dog who needed to visit the emergency vet. We did not have the money for this, and while I was at the vet's office trying to figure out what to do, I called my parents in tears. (Why? I have no idea since my parents are not exactly the comforting type! I think fear and grief clouded my judgment.) I was stunned when my mother said I should take our dog there, and she would cover the bill. Her generosity shocked me, and I did as she said. After our dog was home again several days later and she had paid the bill, for months my mother was especially cruel to me. She called daily and came by our home several times, and every single time, was more vicious than she had been in years. She also did not ask about our dog. Never. I was sure at the time that she paid that bill to give her an excuse to treat me even worse than usual. She knew I would not speak back because she had given me the ability to get our dog the treatment that saved his life. He was absolutely worth every ounce of suffering my mother put me through, but even so, it was still really difficult! If your narcissistic parent offers you money when you are in a bad place, always remember that there will be strings attached to this "gift." It is not done out of kindness or generosity. It is done to give that parent free reign to treat you worse than normal or so they can remind you of what they did for you to make you feel guilty or do something for them.

Many elderly narcissists also like to give away family heirlooms that their children treasure to strangers, friends, other relatives, thrift stores or even throw the items away just to hurt their adult children. If your narcissistic parent has in home health aides, they may receive the things you would like to have, especially if the aides are a good source of narcissistic supply. A bonus for the parent is if you are there at the time that they get rid of the item. They know it hurts you to have to watch that item you always wanted be given to someone else or thrown away, and they enjoy causing you that pain. You need to be aware of the fact that this may happen. Even if you and your narcissistic parent get along well at the moment, you know that can change in the blink of an eye. If at all possible, take pictures of items you treasure, perhaps while your parent is in the bathroom or if you have an excuse to be in their home alone. If your parent is in the hospital, and in need of something from their home, this is a great excuse. Use it! Volunteer to get what they need from their home, and while you are there, take pictures of the items you love. It is best if your parent does not know what you are up to. If they do know, they may want to get rid of the item quickly, even if it had not crossed their mind before to do so.

Along those lines, scan or take pictures of pictures that you want, because they too may go to others or be thrown in the trash rather than given to you. Find time alone to be able to do this as well.

Often, adult children of narcissists receive no inheritance. Narcissists often enjoy hurting their child one last time by providing them with nothing at the end of the parent's life. They may leave everything to a sibling, another relative, friends, or even a charity rather than their adult child (or even grandchildren) just to hurt who they want to hurt. Be prepared that this may happen. Do not count on receiving a nice inheritance to enable you to retire on one day, because it is distinctly possible that may not happen even if your parents are very wealthy.

The telephone may become a weapon to your narcissistic parent as they get older. Sounds strange, right? It is true though. My father in particular uses it. If I do not answer his call, he will call back over and over again in an attempt to force me to answer the phone. A couple of years ago, I think in 2014, he went as far as calling my in–laws (who he knew I had not spoken with since 2002) and one of my cousins who lives about four hundred miles away to tell them to have me call him when I did not answer his call.

Also, if I do not answer the phone on the first ring or two when my parents call, they both have made sarcastic comments to me about assuming I was too busy to talk to them (they think I never have anything to do), or some other snide comment or guilt trip.

And, if I do not take their call, it is a guarantee that the next time I speak with my parents, there will be a guilt trip involved. "I called and called, but you didn't answer! I was so worried about you!" "I just figured you had better things to do than talk to me...." Any rebuttal on my part is met with one of two responses from them. My mother laughs me off and then goes on to talk about herself. My father says almost word for word the same thing every time, "Now, now.. don't you go getting upset."

They also may not answer their phone in order to get attention. After a hospital stay a few years ago, my father had a visiting nurse come by a couple of times each week. One evening, she called me. She said she had been trying to call my parents for about a week to arrange when she could come by, but she never got an answer. I told her I would contact them and call her back. I called my parents, and the same thing happened — I too got no answer. I called repeatedly for a couple of hours, and got no answer. My husband volunteered to stop by their house around eight that evening on his way home from work. Not long before he stopped by, my mother finally called me back. She said, "I saw you called ten times. We were busy." She then went on to tell me about their latest trip to the grocery store, I think it was. Some trivial matter anyway. I rarely called my parents' home, so you would think she would have been concerned I called ten times in a short window of time, but she was not. I explained about the nurse's and my conversation. She said, "Oh yea, I didn't feel like talking to her, so I didn't answer the phone when she called." I scolded my mother for making everyone worry, and this fell on deaf ears. Unfortunately, by doing this, I gave her proof that not answering the phone gains her attention, thus providing narcissistic supply. My husband stopped by while we were on the phone, so she really was happy. She had this nurse and I worried and as a bonus, my husband stopped by out of concern too. She was the center of our worlds for a while, and nothing makes her happier than receiving that much attention.

It amazes me how frustrating a weapon a simple telephone can be in the wrong hands!

To cope, I have some ideas.

Turning off the phone has been helpful, then telling them I need some time to myself or with my husband, so I turned it off. It annoys my parents, but it shows them I have a boundary.

I have told my parents repeatedly please do NOT call me later in the evenings. Nine at night is too late, please call earlier. They both seemed to take this as a challenge. They have called at 8:59 many times. I started ignoring those calls because they were simply pushing boundaries, trying to continue to control the situation.

I also have told my parents do not call early in the morning. Before nine is too early. I need to wake up and do stuff before I am fit to talk to anyone on the phone and be social. I no longer take those early calls.

If I am on the phone with one of my parents and want to hang up, I know that saying, "I need to go" will be completely ignored. Typical of narcissists, they want to control every aspect of the phone call including when we hang up. I had to get creative. If I am on the home phone, I use my cell phone to call my home phone so the call waiting kicks in. I clearly and loudly (so they cannot play the "I didn't hear you" card) say that my call waiting is beeping so I need to go. Another option is to ring my doorbell so my dog starts to bark. I then say, "Did you hear Dixie barking? She's barking because the doorbell rang. I need to go now." In neither situation am I lying. My call waiting did beep and the doorbell did ring. And, these situations work very well. They may help you as well. Several of my readers have told me over the years that they also used these tips with success.

Along the lines of not being able to get off the phone, many times with elderly narcissistic parents, they will do their best to keep their adult child from leaving their presence too soon for their liking. They can make leaving very difficult sometimes, and it can be very frustrating especially since you know it is not because they love you. They only love the supply you provide, which is why they do not want you to leave. There are things you can do to cope with this awkward situation.

As soon as you see your parent, stress that you have to leave by a certain time. As the time is approaching, get ready to go. Remind your parent that you told them you only had until a certain time to visit.

If your narcissistic parent is in an especially vicious mood and although the visit will be brief, you are not sure if you can do it, it is best not to go. If you cannot get out of the visit however, get a friend to help you. Tell your friend ahead of time that you will be visiting your parents at a certain time on a certain date, and ask if she will be available during that time. If so, arrange a signal, such as if you call her and let her phone ring a couple of times (just so your number shows on her caller ID) or send her a blank text. Something you can do easily without being obvious. (You can set your friend's number as a speed dial on your phone or have a blank text ready to send to her with the push of only a button or two.) If your friend receives the signal, she is to call you and say that she needs you to come by immediately – it is an emergency, and she will talk to you about it when you get there. When you get this call, you can tell your parent that an emergency has come up, and you need to go to your friend immediately. Again, you are not lying and neither is your friend. It is an emergency – you need to get away from your narcissistic parent! Your friend is merely helping you to accomplish this.

I have done this, and my mother continued trying to keep me with her instead of leaving. I had to remind her that my friend said it is an emergency, so I need to leave right now. In typical narcissist fashion, someone else's emergency did not matter to her, so I had to force the issue a bit. Basically, I had to make her feel ashamed for not caring about someone's suffering by saying, "I have to go immediately! My friend said it's an emergency, like I said. Don't you care?!" It did work though, and even if my mother was angry at me for leaving her on my terms instead of hers, she knew she could not say anything without looking bad. As you know, looking bad is not something a narcissist can deal with so they will do anything to avoid that.

Some narcissistic parents also will neglect to let you in when you are going by for a visit. They may say they did not hear the doorbell, so they did not answer the door. Or, they may not be home when you are due to stop by, then later they say they forgot you were coming by. You will know if that is true or not. My paternal grandfather once was at the grocery store when my husband and I arrived at his home for a visit one day. He said he did not forget we were coming by, he just wanted to pick up some things at the store so he would have food for us when we came over. My gut said something was very wrong. He never, ever ran out of food and also never, ever forgot when I was coming over. Nothing made sense to me. Not long after, he was diagnosed with Alzheimer's disease. If this had been my narcissistic grandmother instead, for example, I would not have felt that same sense of something wrong. I would have known she had some ulterior motive for not being there.

By not being available when you know they should be, narcissists can keep the attention on them. You will worry that maybe they were taken away in an ambulance, or maybe had a fall and are lying in their home on the floor. They get to be the center of your world for at least a little while. If you have said or done something they did not like, this can be a way to punish you.

Check into the filial duty laws in your state. These laws vary from state to state. In some states, the child of the parent is held legally responsible for providing financially for a destitute parent. You may be expected to pay for your parent's food, clothing, shelter and medical care if they are unable to do so. Or, you may end up with large hospital and medical bills to pay if they move away or after their death.

You also may want to consider getting a life insurance policy on your parent, especially if filial duty laws apply in your state or if you are going to be responsible for their funeral arrangements. It certainly cannot hurt to protect yourself financially.

Many adult children of narcissistic parents that I have spoken with have had chilling stories of visiting them when their parent was dying. The child visited the parent in the hospital close to the end of their life hoping maybe their parent would be different knowing their life was about to end. They asked the parent why they were so cruel or why they did not love the child, and the parent refused to give that child the answers he or she was seeking. Even if such questions were not asked, the narcissistic parent did not show any love or affection to their child. Many narcissistic parents stay bitter and full of hatred for their child until the very end of their lives. Whether or not their adult child was in contact with them seemed to make no difference. Many narcissistic parents were not happy to see their child or wanted to say good bye to them. They said hurtful, terrible things to their child while lying in a hospital bed, dying. Some refused to look at their child or they glared hatefully at their child if they were unable to speak.

Obviously, you do not know what the future will bring, and if your narcissistic parent will behave this way or not at the end of her life. However, I wanted to mention it because apparently this horrible behavior is a very distinct possibility. I am surprised at how common it is, quite frankly. It just goes to show the depths of evil in narcissists.

Narcissism is like a bottomless pit of evil. Narcissistic Personality Disorder is also incredibly destructive to its victims. So often, victims are left empty shells of the person God made them to be, hollow, empty of their own likes, feelings and desires. Yet, in spite of causing so much damage and pain, narcissists often gleefully skip through life, not feeling an ounce of guilt for their horrific behavior.

They often blame their victim or accuse the victim of being the abuser, while saying they are the true victim. In either case, they can garnish a great deal of pity while the true victim is vilified and abandoned. This leads me to believe that Narcissistic Personality Disorder must be demonic in nature. There are evil forces at work in this world, and while I do not believe they are the reason behind every bad thing, I do believe they are at the root of narcissism.

How else could the behaviors of narcissists from various cultures, financial standings and religious beliefs be so incredibly similar while their lives are incredibly different? Here I am in the United States, but I have spoken with people from China, Australia, Africa and other countries whose experiences with narcissists are much like my own.

Also, narcissistic abuse is insidious and its effects are so devastating. It reminds me of what Jesus said in John 10:10, *"The thief cometh not, but for to steal, and to kill, and to destroy: I am come that they might have life, and that they might have it more abundantly."* (Emphasis added) Is this not what narcissistic abuse does to its victims, steals, kills, and destroys? It very often steals, kills and destroys joy, self—esteem, peace, good health and sometimes even sanity.

It is only recently I have begun to think about narcissism in this manner, since I was never one to focus on demonic activity. It has me wondering if God wants me to begin to pray against demons and their activities, and suggesting that others with narcissists in their lives do the same thing.

Spiritual warfare is not a topic in which I am well versed or read, so I hesitate to offer much advice in this area. What I can suggest is if you feel the same as I do about narcissism being demonic in nature, there is nothing wrong with asking God always to protect you and your loved ones against demonic activity. There is also nothing wrong with telling the devil and his evil minions to stay away from you and your family in the name of Jesus. In Luke 10:19—20 Jesus says, *"I have given you authority to trample on snakes and scorpions and to overcome all the power of the enemy; nothing will harm you. [20] However, do not rejoice that the spirits submit to you, but rejoice that your names are written in heaven." (NIV)* Jesus has given those who believe in Him the power to cast out demons, so you certainly can do it. All you have to do is tell them to go away in the name of Jesus. Simple, really.

There is another thing you can do that may help as well especially if your narcissistic parent spends time at your home, but it will at the very least help you even if she does not. Bless your home. I know there are many ways people do this, and frankly I do not know any of the ways. So rather than do a ritual, I have asked God to bless my home. Protect my home, property, cars, and all of us living in my home — human and animal — from evil as well as those who visit my home. I also asked Him to keep out all evil spirits. Years ago, I looked into blessing my home, because there were some unusual paranormal things happening for a short time. None of the rituals felt right to me, so I prayed my own prayer instead. Once I prayed this prayer, the strange things stopped completely, and have not started up again. In fact, several people who have been to my home say how peaceful the atmosphere is in it.

Chapter Three – How To Honor Narcissistic Parents

Every Christian knows Exodus 20:12 says, *"Honour thy father and thy mother: that thy days may be long upon the land which the Lord thy God giveth thee."* Unfortunately, not everyone has good understanding of what honoring parents really means. As a result, there are many, many Christians who were raised by abusive parents who struggle greatly with how to honor their abusive, narcissistic parents.

Merriam–Webster.com defines to honor someone as follows: "a showing of usually merited respect : recognition <pay honor to our founder>"

This does not sound like the way most folks (Christian or not) define honor does it? So many seem to think that to honor your parents or anyone means that you must cater to their every whim and tolerate anything they do to you without a moment's thought of your mental or physical health, your family or your life. Yet, this is completely wrong.

You can honor your narcissistic parent while not tolerating abuse!

Treating your parents with civility and manners is honorable. Disagreeing respectfully, "agreeing to disagree", rather than attempting to force them to accept your views is also honorable.

Helping them when and if you are able is honorable. By helping them, this does not necessarily mean spending hours each day at their home, doing their laundry, bathing them and cooking for them. If you are unable to do such things, there is certainly no shame in that. These days there are many agencies able to provide assistance to the elderly. Contact your local Department of Aging, local churches, Alzheimer's Association, or groups associated with any illness your parent has. Also, visit your local library. Libraries are a wealth of good information, including information on all kinds of organizations in your town, county or state.

Creating boundaries is a very honorable thing to do. Boundaries teach people what is right, what is wrong, and what is and is not acceptable behavior. Enforcing those boundaries in a calm, mature manner is also very honorable, because it encourages people to behave in a good, healthy way. As an example, you can say things like, "I refuse to discuss this with you, and if you continue to talk about it, I'm going to hang up the phone." If they continue, tell them good bye and hang up. If you are new to learning about boundaries, I have a free online course available on my website at: www.CynthiaBaileyRug.com

Catering to your parents' every whim is not honorable. It creates a spoiled and entitled person, and that is not God's will for anyone. Many narcissistic adults were once spoiled children who became entitled and selfish by being catered to as children.

Tolerating abuse and manipulation is not honorable either. Tolerating these awful behaviors basically encourages the abuser to abuse you. The only thing they learn is that abuse gets them what they want, so they should do it all of the time. Basically, tolerating abuse and manipulation encourages someone to sin.

Sometimes even staying away from your parents can be honorable. There is no honor in the situation when your very presence stirs up conflict, or you become very hurt and angry. There are times when creating distance between you and your parents (whether permanently or temporarily) can be the most honorable thing that you can do.

In 2001, I stopped speaking to my mother for several years. I knew in my heart it was necessary, but was unsure if it was honorable. One day, God spoke to my heart saying "Where is the honor in the fact your very presence stirs up strife with your mother?" It made sense to me in that moment that ending our relationship was the most honorable thing I could do at the time. It not only gave me time to heal, learn and grow without her constant presence in my life, but it ended her abusing me by simply removing the opportunity for it to happen. She no longer could sin by abusing me since I removed the opportunity from her. It also showed her that there were consequences for her abusing me.

Chapter Four – Whether Or Not To Go No Contact

Ending any relationship is a very difficult decision, but ending one with your parents, especially in their senior years, is possibly the most difficult decision of all. Abusive or not, they are your parents. You only get one set of those (many of us are very grateful for that fact!). If you divorce your spouse, you can remarry. If you end a friendship, you can make new friends. You cannot go out and get another set of parents though.

These days, so many people have extreme opinions about the topic of no contact with your family but especially your parents. Many people think it is not an option, no matter how cruel and abusive they are. "That's your MOTHER!!" "Your dad won't be around forever yanno!" "He's old, he doesn't know what he's saying." "How much longer will she be around? You need to forgive and forget." All of these are common reactions people have when told that a person has cut a parent out of their life.

Then there are those on the other end of the spectrum who think any small infraction anyone makes, parent or otherwise, that person should be cut out of your life immediately, no questions asked. That mentality has become much more common in the last few years, unfortunately. These people fail to see that no contact should be a last resort, after other efforts have been exercised and failed, rather than a "quick fix" to a relationship problem.

The many people I have talked to who have gone completely no contact with their parents and have no regrets have prayed a great deal, and thought very seriously about their situation before severing ties. They did not tell their parent to get out of their life during the heat of anger. They took a great deal of time to consider everything and pray, then calmly wrote a letter or email to tell their parents of their decision.

Before taking the serious step of going no contact with your narcissistic parent, I urge you to do the same things – pray, and seriously consider your situation. When considering the situation, there are a great many things to think about. Below is a list of some things I believe are vital to considering before going no contact.

- Is the relationship almost always one sided, with you doing all of the giving while the other person does all of the taking?
- Is it affecting your health (mental or physical or both)?
- Have you repeatedly tried to work on the relationship but it either does not improve or gets worse?
- Does your parent accept responsibility for her actions or make excuses for or deny the things she has done?
- Are your boundaries ignored?
- Have you tried going low contact but are still unable to have a civil relationship with your narcissistic parent?

- Do you trust your narcissistic parent?
- Are you afraid of your narcissistic parent?
- Is your narcissistic parent's behavior negatively affecting your marriage and/or children?
- If you opt to go no contact, do you have the strength to continue it no matter what? Can you not contact them no matter what is going on in your life? Can you ignore or return their cards, letters, etc.? If you break no contact, narcissists see this as a sign of weakness. This means you will be treated even worse than prior to going no contact.
- What if, God forbid, your narcissistic parent was to die suddenly? Would you be able to live with yourself knowing your last words were telling her to get out of your life forever?
- What about friends and family? Can you handle them mentioning your narcissistic parent to you, saying she misses you or that you should call her? Are you strong enough to tell them that this topic is not up for discussion, even if it means losing the person from your life?
- What if you wish to keep your other parent in your life? Will that parent automatically side with the one with whom you wish to sever ties or will that parent continue having a relationship with you in spite of the troubles it will cause him or her?
- What about family gatherings? Can you calmly handle seeing your narcissistic parent

there if you are no contact? Would you be able to maintain your peace and dignity and walk away from the get together if that parent was to start any trouble for you?

- What if your parent never changes? Are you capable of continuing the relationship as it has been going indefinitely?
- Would limiting contact be a better option for you at this time? If not permanently, limited contact may be a good stepping stone until you feel you have the strength to go full no contact. Do you think that would be a good solution to your situation at the present time?
- Being completely honest with yourself, what do you feel in your heart is the right decision for you?

I urge you to answer all of these questions with complete honesty and without judging or criticizing yourself. Doing so will help to give you insight on what is best for you to do in this painful situation.

Also I urge you not to let anyone else tell you what you should do. Getting input from those who know you and the situation is fine, but never blindly follow someone's advice. They are answering from their own experiences and beliefs which may be different than yours. They may feel much differently about things than you do, so their advice may not work for you. And, if the person knows your parent, they will answer your question while keeping your parent's feelings in mind. (This person is definitely not someone you should discuss your thoughts with regarding possibly severing ties with your parent!) Certainly consider the input of others if it makes sense, but if any part of it does not feel right for you, then do not do it.

If you have any doubts about going no contact, then I urge you to hold off until you feel the time is right to do so. Do not misunderstand me – I certainly am for going no contact, as often it is the only solution for victims of narcissistic abuse. However, if you have any doubts, then there has to be a good reason for it. Low contact may be a good option for you at this time.

Low contact is just as it sounds, you have low contact with your narcissistic parent. You only take their calls or see them when you feel able to do so. You have very strong boundaries in place on the times you do interact with them. You keep the relationship on a very superficial level, not discussing personal details or anything that could be used to hurt you. Instead you discuss your parent, the weather or any other light topic. The Gray Rock Method is firmly in place, and your best friend.

Low contact has no time limit. You can use it as a stepping stone to going full no contact, or you can continue the relationship with your narcissistic parent like this indefinitely. I have known people who have used it in both ways successfully. It is a very good alternative if you want to go no contact, but have doubts. It gives you some space and time away from your parent to clear your mind. That space also allows you to pray, heal, learn and grow without your parent being a constant distraction. Some narcissistic parents get upset enough by low contact to improve their behavior, although sadly this is not a common occurrence.

In any case, low contact should be a valid option if you have any doubts about going no contact. If you have doubts, if something just does not feel right about no contact, there is a reason for it, and you need to trust that.

As I mentioned before, I too went no contact with my mother in 2001. I prayed and thought about things for quite some time before writing the letter to my mother to tell her I wanted her out of my life. It was not easy, but I did it once I felt complete peace with my decision. That peace enabled me to follow through with what I knew I needed to do, as hard as it was.

I did allow my mother back in my life in 2007 when she called me after having heart surgery. I felt stronger and able to handle a relationship again after six years apart for me to heal. And, I naively thought she had changed after coming close to death. Obviously, I knew nothing of Narcissistic Personality Disorder at the time, so I did not realize the changes were only temporary. In spite of that, this time, things were different between us. Better for sure but not great. They never will be great with a narcissist unless they genuinely want to improve their behavior, and make appropriate changes.

In 2015, I began wanting both my mother and my father out of my life. I nearly died that February, and I realized I could not tell my parents about what had happened to me. They would turn my problem back to them, and ignore both my physical and emotional pain as well as the new symptoms I now live with. It made me angry, because I realized how fed up I was with knowing I could not count on my parents for any support or concern. I wanted them out of my life. However, something odd happened. I knew in my heart, beyond a shadow of a doubt, that it was not good for me to tell them any of this. I had no explanation for how I felt, but I knew enough to listen to my instincts in spite of people telling me I should just tell my parents how I felt, that I wanted to be no contact, and get it over with. It was very difficult, because I felt like a hypocrite. I tell people in my books and blog that there is nothing wrong with going no contact, yet I was unable to do so myself. That is not a nice way to feel!

Then on April 30, 2016, my husband's mother passed away. Two days later, one of our cats suddenly passed away. (Losing a pet is always devastating for me since they are much like my children.) The next day, our internet and phone went out. When they were repaired a couple of days later, the first call we got was from my father. I prayed quickly, asking God to guide my words, then answered the phone. He told me that he and my mother saw my mother in–law's obituary in the local paper, as I knew they would. He was obviously upset I had not told my parents, and said they would have attended her funeral, but now it was too late.

I was completely taken aback. I knew when my parents found out about her death, I would get a call. I assumed it would be to say they were sorry to hear that my husband's mother had passed, she was such a wonderful person, my mother's back hurt too badly to attend her funeral then she would regale me with her latest woes about her bad back. Actually wanting to attend her funeral was totally unexpected, and it caught me completely off guard. I asked my father why they wanted to go and he said to pay their respects of course. I was livid at this point, and let him know that in no uncertain terms. I reminded him that my mother in–law hated me from the day we met, and never even tried to hide that fact from me. I told him that she was very abusive and cruel to me, and I was hurt they wanted to pay respects to someone who abused me like she did. My father said that was my husband's mother, and I said that did not give her the right to abuse me. We argued more, he back peddled some, changed the subject, then eventually asked if my husband was home. I said not yet, he was still at work. "Oh. Your mother wants to talk to him." I said too bad, because he was not home. "I guess she'll have to talk to you then." He sounded very disappointed in that no one could talk to my husband. My mother then got on the phone, and said how sorry she was to hear of my mother in–law's passing, and how they would have attended her funeral if they had only known in time, saying almost the same things my father said. I blew up again, repeating almost the exact same things I had said to my father. She asked if I would have been mad if they went and I said absolutely. That is betraying me! That woman hated me! There would be no reason for you to go to her funeral! My mother's comeback was "But that's Eric's mother!" I said, "But I'm your DAUGHTER!" She was not hearing anything I said. She reminded me a couple more times that was his mother so I reminded her back that I was her daughter and I felt completely betrayed that she and my father had more respect for a stranger, someone they have seen only twice since my husband and I got together in 1994, than me. My cries and even cursing fell on deaf ears. My mother said things like she could not hear me (she has hearing problems, but she also exaggerates it when it benefits her) until I was screaming into the phone. Then she eventually went silent. She silently listened to me yelling with only the occasional bored sigh to let me know she was still on the phone. I finally told her I am done. I am not discussing this topic with her a moment longer so if she had anything else to say, just say it before I hang up. She started complaining about a minor health issue she has, and that was the final straw for me. She wanted my sympathy after hurting me! I could not do it and let her know I really did not care about her minor issue. We ended up basically hanging up on each other at that point.

My mother called a couple of evenings later to speak with my husband to offer her condolences. I have not heard from her since other than an anniversary card then later a Christmas card she sent my husband and I. My father halfheartedly apologized a few days after our fight. He called I think I counted seventeen times in two days until he woke me before seven one morning, basically tricking me into answering the phone by calling while I was asleep. He calls sometimes but not often, and we are never on the phone for more than ten minutes at the most. He used to keep me on the phone for at least a half an hour.

When this first happened, I was completely baffled. I told God how sorry I was for blowing up at my parents. I was ashamed of how I yelled and cussed at them. I did not understand what I did wrong. I prayed before answering, which always has meant I stayed calm no matter what. What happened this time? Was I so easily upset because I was already feeling emotionally fragile after losing one of our cats? Was it because they caught me completely off guard by wanting to attend my mother in—law's funeral? I asked God about it repeatedly over the next few months. At first, He wanted me to focus on grieving my loss. He told me to mentally put my parents in a box on a shelf, and deal with them once I felt better. I did, and am glad I did. I was able to grieve losing my little girl in peace. Once I was in a better place emotionally, God finally spoke to my heart one day, and gave me my answer.

He told me that He wanted my parents to see me so upset. He wanted them to know that their hurtful actions turned their normally calm, reasonable daughter into a cursing, screaming maniac. No, it would not make them apologize for hurting me, but He wanted my parents to see it anyway, as it would make them want to avoid me. He also later told me that He does not want me to tell them I want to be no contact. Instead, He wants me to stay low contact for now, not contacting them, focusing on my healing, setting my boundaries when I interact with them and calling them out on their cruelty. This behavior will make my parents want to stay away from me naturally, because I am not so easy to push around any longer. If I were to initiate no contact, it would not go well for me, He said. The flying monkeys would come out of the woodwork, shaming me for abandoning my elderly parents when they need me the most, and I would feel incredibly guilty, even knowing it was for the best. I could be sucked back into a relationship with them, which would be harder on me than ever. And, interestingly, when I told a friend of mine about this, she suggested that maybe also God wants me to be blameless before Him and man as well. If my parents refuse to speak to me, how can I be to blame for "abandoning" them when they are the ones who have chosen not to speak to me?

God's answer has given me a great deal of peace. I also realize that by doing things His way, I am much bolder and less afraid of calling my parents out on their abuse. Although I have not had the chance of doing so with my mother, I have no doubt I will be able to do so if the situation arises. I have done it with my father with no trouble, so I believe can do it with my mother as well.

My situation is rather unique, I know. I have not heard of anyone in a similar one, but that does not mean it is only me who has been in such a position. That is why I am including it in this book, because I am sure there are others who God has told to allow their narcissistic parent to be the one to go no contact rather than them. If that is you, Dear Reader, I am sorry. I know it is an incredibly challenging position to be in at best. I also know that God has reasons for everything, and this situation is no different. Please trust Him to lead you down the right path. Proverbs 3:5–6 *"⁵ Trust in the Lord with all thine heart; and lean not unto thine own understanding. ⁶ In all thy ways acknowledge him, and he shall direct thy paths."*

Chapter Five — To Help Or Not To Help Your Elderly Narcissistic Parent?

If you continue your relationship with your narcissistic parent, the issue whether or not you will help them as their health declines is going to become an issue.

When narcissistic parents age and need assistance, many factors are involved in whether or not to help them. How high on the spectrum are your narcissistic parents? Do you feel strong enough to deal with them on what could possibly be a daily basis? Do you have the time to help them while maintaining your own family and job?

Chances are, you are going to struggle a lot with the decision, especially if you have been low or no contact with your parents for a while. On the good side, this shows your humanity and good heart. If you did not have these good qualities, it would be easy for you to turn your back on them. In spite of trying to destroy you, your narcissistic parents did not destroy your caring heart!

No one should tell you what to do in this situation, but chances are, at least one person will try to. Unless you asked for that person's opinion, it is usually best to ignore their input. Instead, pray. Ask God for wisdom and to show you what you should do. James 1:5 says,

"If any of you lack wisdom, let him ask of God, that giveth to all men liberally, and upbraideth not; and it shall be given him." And Proverbs 2:6 says, *"For the LORD giveth wisdom: out of his mouth cometh knowledge and understanding."* Obviously God is very willing to help, so why not ask Him to? Not one time in my life that I have asked God for wisdom has He disappointed me. In fact, He has given me some great ideas and some very creative ones too when I needed them. He will do the same for you, all you have to do is ask.

Also, you are an adult now. You have the right to decide whether or not to help your parents, and if so, in what ways you can help them. Remember that!

Do NOT allow your narcissistic parents to guilt trip you into taking care of them because they are your parents, because you owe them, because they changed your diapers when you were a baby, because they fed and clothed you. You did not ask to be born nor did you ask them to take care of you, so such arguments are invalid.

Consider the state of your healing before deciding whether or not to help your parents. You simply cannot help them in a hands on manner if you are not at a decent place of healing. You automatically will fall into old, dysfunctional habits and patterns easily if you are not in a good place emotionally and mentally. Dealing with your narcissistic parents can be a huge trigger. It not only can trigger flashbacks and repressed memories, but it can force you to behave in old dysfunctional behaviors out of sheer habit. If you have Post Traumatic Stress Disorder (PTSD) or Complex Post Traumatic Stress Disorder (C—PTSD) due to being raised by at least one narcissistic parent (like so many of us do), these triggers can be especially difficult for you. If you opt to help your parents, you need to be in a place where you realize you have rights too, your self—esteem needs to be healing and you need to have a good, healthy grasp on having and enforcing healthy boundaries.

You also need to have accepted the fact that your parents are narcissists, and they likely will not get better. While it is true that with God all things are possible, and it is great to pray and hope they will change, you need to accept that they may not, or that they may get worse. It is not because God cannot change them, but because God will not force people to do things, even if it is in their best interest to do so. If the narcissist is closed off to God as many are, they may completely ignore His promptings and efforts to get their attention. Or, they may sense something is going on, and get angry about it.

Often, bringing in elder care or having your narcissistic parent move into an assisted living facility is the best situation for everyone involved. Your parents will get good care, and you will not be expected to take care of them every moment of every day. If you can, find out if your parents have long term care insurance to help with the cost of in home care or have investments or assets that can pay for it or assisted living.

Chapter Six – Being Your Narcissistic Parents' Caregiver

If you are absolutely certain that you can handle caring for your elderly narcissistic parent, you do not have an easy road ahead of you. The year I spent taking care of my narcissistic grandmother was possibly the most difficult of my life. It taught me plenty about Narcissistic Personality Disorder, even though I never had heard of it at the time.

The first thing you need to remember to do is pray. Pray often. In fact, pray all of the time. God is there for you and will support you. Ask Him for wisdom, insight, strength, comfort and anything else you need to help you get through this challenging time, and trust He will provide you with whatever you need.

Learn to see things through your narcissistic parent's eyes. I know this can be hard when you are not a narcissist, but if you can do it, it will help you in many ways. You will understand fully that their behavior is not necessarily about you, but instead about how dysfunctional your parent is. They are trying to hurt you to make themselves feel better, or manipulate you in order to gain control and feel powerful. Truly understanding things like this enables you to deal with these behaviors effectively as well as not be so hurt since you realize they are truly not the personal attacks that they feel like. You also can create new and effective ways to deal with your narcissistic parent when you really understand how they see things.

Seeing things from their perspective also may help you to understand their concerns better. Sometimes the things that concern a caregiver are not important to the one being cared for, or vice versa. Seeing their side can help you to have a better grasp of the situation at hand, which means you can provide better care. And, if you have concerns, write them down to discuss with either your parent or doctor at an appropriate time.

Always remember, with narcissists, it is always ALL about them. Everything. Always. All the time, without a break, ever. If you need something from your parent, phrase it in a way that your parent will benefit from it rather than how you will. You will stand a much better chance at getting it if they do not realize it benefits you, but instead believe it will benefit them. If you are in need of your parent to do something to make caring for them easier for you, do NOT say that! Instead, word your request so it sounds like it will benefit your parent, not you. Narcissists will be much more open to making changes or spending money on something that will benefit them than you. Leave your own needs, thoughts, opinions and feelings out of the discussion as much as possible, and focus instead on your parent and her needs. It is the best way you can have success in this area.

Figure out ways to protect yourself against any accusations your narcissistic parent may come up with. Written documentation is always good (such as doctor's notes, receipts from stores, etc), as are witnesses whenever possible. Since many narcissists are quite extroverted, your parent may enjoy having company often. Encourage that so there are others who see the things you do, and will learn what kind of person you are. That way, they will not believe your narcissistic parent's lies about you if the opt to create a smear

49

campaign against you at some point. Even when you do not care what others think of you, smear campaigns are a huge nuisance.

When caring for your narcissistic parents, always remember that you do not have to ask "how high" when they tell you to jump. You have rights! You also deserve to be treated with respect and civility.

If you need to confront your parents on their actions, do so in a calm manner. **No matter a narcissist's age or whether they are overt or covert, never show them that you are upset.** This feeds them narcissistic supply, which you never, ever want to do. The more supply you feed a narcissist, the more they will want, even demand, from you.

Always remember to maintain realistic expectations with your narcissistic parent. Release the expectation that because they are elderly or infirmed that suddenly they will have a moment of clarity, realize what they have done and apologize to you for everything. Also release the expectation that this time will be better, because chances are it will not be. Having unrealistic expectations will only lead to great disappointment and sadness for you when it does not happen.

Remember too that no matter their age, narcissists are manipulative. They can and will use their failing health to manipulate. They may use it to gain sympathy and attention or to attempt to make you feel guilty enough to do things for them. Manipulation and control are just a part of what they do, and that will not improve just because they need to rely on your assistance now.

If other family members are helping your narcissistic parent as well as you, be prepared for your parent to attempt to pit you and the others against each other. In my situation with my narcissistic grandmother, as I mentioned, I lived closest to her so she called me more than anyone. However, my mother, aunt and cousins helped out as well when they were able to. My one cousin in particular really tried to help out our grandmother, but she was limited in her ability to do so. She lived about ninety minutes away and did not drive. She had to get a ride to the train station, then take the train to the station about one mile from our grandmother's house, then walk the rest of the way. The procedure was done in reverse in the evening to go home. (Side note: to the best of my knowledge, our grandmother never offered to pay for her train tickets.) When I was with our grandmother, she told me constantly about what a good job this cousin did. She said things like, "She does that so much better than you do." "That's not how she does it – you should ask her how she does it so you can do it that way too." "She's always doing for me. I don't know what I'd do without her." "She's the only one who I can always count on." I spent a lot of time angry about this until one day when I was alone with my cousin. We started talking about caring for our grandmother. It turned out that our grandmother said the exact same things to her about me! I believe our grandmother also did this same thing with our mothers when they were growing up, which is probably why they never got along. Trying to pit us against each other made both my cousin and I work harder to please our grandmother, and kept enough resentment between us to prevent us from discussing this situation for a long time. This is a common tactic of narcissists since it works very well for them. It certainly worked well for my grandmother! My grandmother's two daughters have barely spoken in the last forty years. I am grateful my cousin and I figured out what was happening! At least we do not hate each other like our mothers seem to.

You also will need to remember that no matter how much you do or how well you do things, it will never be enough for a narcissist. They are impossible to please. If you manage to please them, suddenly they will want something different, deny they wanted that in the first place or say they want it, but you did it wrong and need to do it a different way. They love to put people in the situation of being able to do nothing right in their eyes because it makes that person work harder and harder to please the narcissist.

As with any caregiving situation, there are going to be emergencies. Unlike your average caregiving situation, some emergencies will be real, some will be a cry for attention. As usual, ask

God for wisdom, discernment and whatever else you need to handle the crisis at hand.

Always remember not to reward bad behavior. If the crisis is a cry for attention, do not provide it or they will continue to do things like this. As soon as you see that the crisis at hand is not a genuine crisis, respond accordingly. Remain calm, show no emotion and state whatever facts you need to say.

Sometimes, things will be even more difficult than normal and you will have to take charge. These are extremely challenging times, but they are unavoidable when you are a caregiver. You may need to call 911 when they do not want you to because you know you cannot handle this crisis. You may need to force one parent to visit the other in the hospital in order to find out what is happening with the patient. I did this with my mother when my father was in the hospital in 2014. My mother refused to visit him, claiming with her bad back, she could not walk to his room since the hospital is rather large. I told my mother I would be at her house at a specific time, so get dressed, we are going to the hospital. They have wheelchairs we could borrow, so she would be fine. Not nice, but also necessary as the staff would not share details of my father's condition with me, only my mother.

You may even need to take them to the doctor when they do not want to go, forcing them to get ready to go and then forcing them into the car. I had to do this once with my grandmother, and it was not fun. It was also necessary as she had shattered her shoulder a few days prior and was told she needed to see a doctor a couple of days after leaving the hospital. She did not want to go since she was not feeling well, but she had to go to find out what further care was needed. She was mad at me at first, especially when I broke the speed limit driving her car to get her there on time, but she did see the doctor as she needed to do.

Times like these are difficult, but they can be managed. Stay strong. Remind yourself you are doing this thing for them for a good reason, and they have no choice but to go along with you. You are not hurting them. Quite the opposite in fact, you are helping them, so take charge knowing you are doing the right thing.

Look into your state's Power of Attorney laws. Your parent may want you to assume that role at some point, so you are wise to plan ahead, understanding what all this involves. Basically, being someone's Power of Attorney means you are legally allowed to act on their behalf. Many seniors wish to have one of their children act as their Power of Attorney. It also may become a necessity if your parent has dementia or Alzheimer's, due to their diminished mental capabilities.

You also may need to learn about your parent's finances. What investments do they have and where? What banks do they use? Do they have life insurance? Long term care insurance? These are things you will need to know if your parent's health declines to the point of needing to move into assisted living or a nursing home.

It is a good idea to learn what you can about your parent's will and final wishes. This is a hard topic to bring up, but especially with narcissists. You must try to talk about it, at least, even if they shut you down. It is important that you know things like what their wishes are, such as their end of life care, what they wish to bequeath to whom after their death, do they wish to be buried or cremated, do they wish to donate their organs and more. Some states' attorney general's offices offer forms you need on their website or you can have mailed to you free of charge. Having the forms you need in hand could help you to start the conversation with your parent.

Once the forms are completed, keep them in a safe location, such as a lock box. It is a good idea to place a copy of them in a prominent place in your parent's home, such as on the refrigerator. That is often where paramedics look for vital information. Also be certain your parent keeps a copy with her if she travels and provides a copy to her primary care doctor, any other doctors or specialists she sees, you, any other close family members and a spiritual leader if she likes.

You can have your parent's needs assessed. A social worker can come to your parent's home, and determine what her needs are, and

53

what services are available to her. If money is tight, the social worker can guide you and your parent to free or low cost help. Contact your local Department of Social Services for more information.

Develop a relationship as best you can with your parent's doctors. Be open and honest with them so your parents cannot con the doctors. I remember taking my grandmother to her primary care doctor many times. For some reason, she usually wanted me to go into the exam room with her rather than me staying in the waiting room. She would tell the doctor that her issues were worse than they really were, so he would listen to her, then ask me how she was really doing. I could provide insight that she would not admit to, which helped him to provide her with accurate care.

Doctors are not obligated to tell you anything about your parent's health, even if the parent gives permission, although some will. Even so, they are obligated to listen to what you have to say about your parents, and hopefully will add notes to their files.

If you prefer, make an appointment to see the doctor when you are alone so your parents will not be a distraction. This may be a very good option for you.

When visiting the doctor with your narcissistic parent, always keep a current list of medications (prescription and over the counter), vitamins and any other supplements she takes with you. Your parent may not keep track of them, so you do it in case she does not.

One very common and painful task associated with caring for elderly parents is when it is time to take the car keys. I have become very concerned about my father in this area, so I looked into what can be done here in Maryland. Apparently, if you have the person's driver's license number, you can report them to the Department of Motor Vehicles, and they will look into the situation. I am not sure what other states follow that same procedure. You need to check into that in your particular state. Or, you can talk to your parent's doctor (or doctors) about the situation without your parent's knowledge.

No one wants to hear that they should surrender their driver's license, so it is a very difficult situation even under the best of circumstances. Narcissists, as always, make a difficult situation much worse. It is best if at all possible to arrange for a doctor to talk to your parent about this topic. Most narcissists seem to respect doctors, often blindly listening to what they have to say.

If you must have the driving discussion with your parent however, remember to keep the topic on your parent. Driving is dangerous for your parent, she may get hurt, she may wreck her car, an accident would cost her a lot of money, and similar comments will make the narcissist listen. Saying you are afraid she will cause an accident that will hurt other people however? No narcissist will listen to that argument, because other people mean nothing to narcissists. They only care about themselves, so keep the focus on your parent as much as humanly possible in order to have a successful and productive conversation.

Everyone needs to feel useful, so involve your narcissistic parent in daily activities as much as possible. When a person does not feel useful, it can lead to depression. Think of how useless you feel if you have the flu or a broken leg and cannot do your normal tasks. It makes you feel sad, doesn't it? If that feeling was permanent, it would be much more depressing. That is how it can be for the elderly. It is best to avoid this awful feeling so the person does not become depressed. A narcissist may become depressed and angry, and if they become angry, you as the caregiver could be the target. It is best to avoid that if at all possible.

Granted, someone very elderly or infirmed probably cannot do a lot, but they usually can do some small tasks. When caring for my narcissistic grandmother, she wanted applesauce one day. I assumed this meant she had a jar on the shelf, but I was wrong. She did not mean that. She wanted homemade. She taught me how to make it, and helped me to peel and core the apples. It turned into a surprisingly pleasant afternoon. My grandmother told me some stories about her family as we worked together, and seemed to enjoy herself. It was the only really nice time she and I had together, maybe partly because she felt useful.

When providing a task for your parent, do so with respect. "Please" and "Thank you" will go a long way, as will asking her to do something rather than telling her to do something.

There is nothing wrong with asking your narcissistic parent for help, either. It will make her feel useful as well as help you if she can do some smaller tasks. She probably can write checks for paying her bills, go through her mail, peel potatoes for dinner or other small tasks. You know what your parent is and is not capable of doing, so use that information wisely.

If your narcissistic parent likes to cook or bake, maybe ask her to help you in the kitchen, or to show you how she makes a certain dish. (Some narcissists guard their recipes with their life, so you need to know if your narcissistic parent is that way. If so, she may become angry with you for wanting her "secret" recipe, and refuse to share it. If that happens, just drop the subject.) You also could ask her to teach you some other skill, such as how to knit or some other craft. Narcissists love to show off their skills, so this will make them happy as well as teach you a new skill. It also may create a surprisingly pleasant experience with your parent as making applesauce with my grandmother did for me.

Never, ever forget who you are dealing with. Always keep in mind the fact that your parent is a narcissist who knows you very well. She knows what buttons to push and what ways to control you work best. Do not forget these things will be used. Recognize them when they are used, and do not fall for the games.

You have a life and a schedule too, so work on creating something that works for you, not only your parent. Make sure when she schedules appointments, the appointment fits into your schedule if you are going to have to take her to it. If she does do not like that, she is more than welcome to find someone else to help whose schedule works better with hers than yours does. Remind her of that little fact, calmly of course.

Keep a calendar or appointment book handy so your parent knows what to expect on what day, and keep a matching one for yourself. If possible, use a calendar app on your cell phone and your parent's cell phone or computer that can sync, so you both have matching information at all times. Mark doctor appointments, social engagements, dates to refill prescriptions and anything else you can think of on the calendar. The more that is on the calendar, the better for you, as it means less that you will need to remember, thus relieving some of your stress. It also will help to avoid any mix ups when things are written on a calendar. Do not forget to mark certain times when you will not be available at all, and make sure your parent knows on those days, she must contact someone else if she needs assistance. You could write something like this on the calendar: "March 5 – Sally is not available until the following morning. Call Tom instead at (555) 555—5555 if needed." You will need the breaks, and your narcissistic parent needs to respect that, like it or not. If she does not, you can turn your phone off or even block her number for the day.

It is also good idea is to have a key to your parent's home. This way if, God forbid, your parent is unable to come to the door, you still can get into the house. Also it is a convenience for them. I had one to my grandmother's home, so I could let myself in without bothering her. She did not need to rush to the door to let me in. She knew what time I was coming over, so when I got there, I would knock on the door, then let myself in.

If you help your narcissistic parent pay their bills or if you pay them yourself, keep a written record of what was paid on what date, check numbers, transaction confirmation codes and anything else so there can be no doubt that you used their money for its intended purpose. You do not want your narcissistic parent to accuse you of stealing from them! There are budgeting computer programs available that may be of help to you. Or, simply use a bookkeeper's or accountant's log book.

Along these lines, if you go out alone to buy things for your narcissistic parent, always get receipts. Money is extremely important to narcissists. For many, it is their god. They need to have clearly written evidence that you are spending only what they wanted you to spend, on what they wanted it spent on. It also protects you against them claiming you are stealing their money.

Always remember your boundaries and have creative ways to enforce them in your calmest demeanor. Chances are good this is going to anger your narcissistic parent, but that is not your responsibility. Setting healthy boundaries is very reasonable, but that will not stop them from trying to force you to stop those boundaries. Suddenly, they may regale you with stories about how their cousin's daughter takes her mother to Bingo every Tuesday evening, or how their friend's son just bought her a brand new 47" television and even hooked it up for her just because he loves his mother. The goal of these stories is much like my grandmother's goal in pitting my cousin and I against each other – to make you feel inferior, so you will try harder and harder to please the narcissist. Do not let that get to you! Show no emotion when the stories happen. In fact, you can say something simple like, "That's nice." Or "Good for them." Then casually change the subject, acting as if their story or snide comments did not hurt or anger you. Once you are out of your parent's presence however, get those feelings out of you! You do not need the bitterness inside of you.

When a narcissist decides to amp up their rage, it will get creative and can be absolutely horrible. My mother has done this to me, and I was simply amazed. Actually I still am even years later! A couple of years ago, I was temporarily doing my parents' laundry while my father was recovering from a stroke, as my mother says her back pain prevents her from doing laundry. Before I went over one day, I called first to set up what time I should arrive. During the conversation with my mother, she mentioned how her bowels had been acting up. She had messed herself twice and I needed to wash the clothes. The next words she said will always amaze me. Before I had the opportunity to say anything, she quickly said, "I changed your diaper when you were a baby, so you owe it me to do this!"

When I went to my parents' home later that day, I went with rubber gloves in case I had to touch her clothing. At first, I did not. She handed me a small laundry bag with dirty clothes, so I simply dumped the clothes in the washer. After going upstairs, and while not wearing the rubber gloves, my mother greeted me and said, "Hold out your hand." I did and she put her nasty, filthy clothes in my hand. She smiled really big, and said, "I forgot – these need to go in that load too. Run that downstairs to the washer." Mind you, my mother knows I am not good at all with body functions, yet she deliberately put her dirty, poopy clothes in my bare hand. My stomach churned for the rest of the day, and she was extremely happy with herself. I honestly do not even remember why she was angry with me, but she was obviously VERY angry to stoop to such a low, foul and simply disgusting level.

When you are a full or part time caregiver, people can be very kind. They may tell you what a good daughter or son you are for taking care of your elderly parent. It is a lovely thing to hear, unless it is said in front of your narcissistic parent. Since narcissists must remain the center of attention, heaping all praise and admiration unto themselves, you receiving even a simple complement can be quite a narcissistic injury to them. Since you received the complement, thus being the reason for the narcissistic injury, then you must receive their wrath. At least that is how their minds work. (Isn't narcissistic logic amazing, and not in a good way?) I was in a store with my narcissistic grandmother once when an employee saw us. He asked me if this was my grandmother (we looked nothing alike), and I said yes. He told me what a good granddaughter I was to take her shopping and how God would bless me for being so good to her. It was so nice to hear, especially since she always acted like she was doing me a favor by allowing me to help her, but my grandmother got mad. She was I think eighty–four years old at the time, very small and frail, yet managed to stomp off angrily as the gentleman was talking. She was also especially nasty to me for the rest of my time with her that day. My mother is exactly like her mother in this way. If someone says something nice to me in her presence, she gets downright hateful and cruel to me for a while afterwards. This type of scenario is very common among narcissists, especially elderly ones, so be prepared for it. You cannot stop a person from saying something, of course, but you can prepare yourself for the ugly narcissistic rage that will follow. You will know what to expect from your past experiences with your narcissistic parent. The silent treatment, more vicious criticisms than usual, bragging about someone who does more for their parent than you do, or someone who is more successful than you... all of these are common ways for elderly narcissists to vent their rage.

You will be talked about by your narcissistic parent even more than usual if you are in a caregiving role, and chances are, it will not be good. How you provide care and what you do may be criticized. Your narcissistic parent may complain that you do not do enough to other people. She may even create totally bizarre things to tell others about you. My narcissistic grandmother told my aunt that she could not get rid of me. She claimed I stayed at her house so often to hide from my husband, because our marriage was so bad. My aunt, who did not know me well, approached me when we were alone in my grandmother's kitchen one day and asked how things were with my husband. I said things were fine, why? She told me what my grandmother said, and I was stunned. I pointed out to her I spent time with my grandmother while my husband was at work. If I was hiding from him, shouldn't I wait until he gets home to go to her house? My aunt could not deny the logic. I am unsure why neither she nor I confronted my grandmother about this bizarre lie, but we really should have.

If your narcissistic parent talks about you behind your back, I know it is frustrating. Try to ignore the stupidity of it the best you can, and tell people the truth (calmly, not in a defensive way) when it makes sense to do so. If people start criticizing how you do things, listen to what they say. If they have a valid point, make the appropriate changes as you see fit. However, if they are simply repeating nonsense said by your narcissistic parent, ignore their foolishness the best you can, and vent about it later to someone safe. You can respond to them by saying things like, "You're entitled to your opinion." "We'll just have to agree to disagree." Or, you simply can change the subject.

Never forget that your narcissistic parent is not the only one who needs care. You need it too, especially since you are a caregiver! Never neglect to take care of yourself. Caregiving is an absolutely arduous task even under the best of circumstances. Taking care of a narcissistic parent or two? Incredibly grueling, even on the best days. Spend time alone with God. Take breaks as often as you can. Spend time with loving and supportive people who understand your situation. Counseling may be a good idea as well if you can find a counselor local to you who understands Narcissistic Personality Disorder. Not many counselors were taught a great deal about narcissism or other cluster B personality disorders, believe it or not. It may take seeing a few counselors before finding the right one for you who has a good understanding of Narcissistic Personality Disorder and the damage it can cause victims.

If your narcissistic parent has Alzheimer's or dementia, you are no doubt facing an especially difficult challenge. Learn everything you can about your parent's condition, and what to expect as the disease progresses. There are many websites on the topics that can help you, as well as your local Alzheimer's association.

One thing you need to know about if you are caring for someone with Alzheimer's or dementia is many people stress keeping an Alzheimer's or dementia patient in reality. Personally, I think that depends on the patient. I spent quite a bit of time taking my narcissistic grandmother to visit her husband in the nursing home, which means I also spent time with people with advanced Alzheimer's during those visits. I noticed that when they were forced to accept reality, it frustrated many of them. Yet, going along with their delusion kept them more peaceful. For example, one gentleman thought I was his daughter. I let him think it, since it seemed to make him happy. He must have adored his daughter, judging by how happy he was thinking I was her. In a few moments, I suppose the delusion stopped, and he simply walked away. At least he was happy for a few moments, spending time with his "daughter." I wish I had been able to meet her, and tell her how much he loved her! She needed to know that.

A few years ago, my father was in the hospital with a spinal injury. He was in extreme pain, and very over medicated on pain medications. He became delusional as a result. I thought about the gentleman with Alzheimer's I just mentioned, and just went along with whatever he thought was going on at the time. My mother, however, often would correct my father and I. Each time she did that, he would get angry and frustrated. One day, when my father called me, "Mom," I went along with it. He was fighting getting proper care, so while he thought I was his mother, I called him the nickname my grandmom called him, then told him to behave or else I was going to smack him. (No, I would not have smacked him, but he did not know that at the moment. Grandmom was a tough lady, and she might have smacked him, so I just played that card!) He did, and gave me no more problems after that. Judging from that experience, I have to conclude that going along with the patient's delusions can be beneficial in situations like my father was in when overmedicated, too. It requires quick thinking, discernment and wisdom to decide if that would work in your individual situation.

It may happen that you feel the time to go no contact with your parent is now, while you are taking care of them. It is understandable, really. If this happens, you are going to need God's wisdom like never before on how to go about doing it. God may deal with you in a unique way to do this, as He has me. (I told my story in chapter four about going no contact, so I will not repeat it here). If God suddenly starts to deal with you more than usual about healing, growing stronger with setting and enforcing your boundaries, maybe He is helping you to go no contact in the same manner as He did me, by basically becoming someone healthy, who your narcissistic parent will push away.

You also will need to be prepared if you go no contact no matter how you do it, because the narcissist may become exceptionally volatile. They may initiate a smear campaign, trashing you to anyone and everyone for abandoning your "poor, elderly, helpless" parent. Relatives and friends may not understand and criticize you. They may try to "talk some sense" into you by trying to make you feel guilty for your decision. They may tell you that your parent misses you, is depressed or even suicidal without you. These people who are saying these things to you, are they talking about any clear evidence that your parent has changed? Or, is it the same old, same old – guilt, manipulation, etc.? If you see or hear no evidence at all of change, then I would strongly urge you to avoid contacting that parent! If you allow them to manipulate you back into their life, things will get even worse for you. They may behave briefly, but it will not last. When the good behavior ends, watch out, because you will see a narcissistic rage like you have never seen before.

Think of the situation from your parent's perspective, through the very warped perspective of a narcissist: you unfairly abandoned her in her time of great need for no reason whatsoever, and now you want to come crawling back into her life. You should be punished for your awful actions! You said you wanted your parent out of your life, then you wanted her back in your life. Obviously your mind can be changed, and your weak boundaries mean nothing. They can be trampled over easily enough. This makes you easy to control.

Granted, this "logic" makes no sense to someone who is not a narcissist, so it can be hard to wrap your mind around. However, if you are a narcissist like your parent, this thinking makes perfect sense. Remember it if you go no contact and are considering breaking that, especially if you severed ties while caring for your parent.

Chapter Seven – Caregiving From A Distance

If you live far from your parent or opt not to participate in a hands on caregiver role with your elderly narcissistic parent, there is absolutely no shame in that. It is a very challenging thing to do, being a caregiver, and not everyone is able to do it due to countless very valid reasons, even if their parent is not a narcissist.

As usual, I recommend prayer as the first place for you to start. God can help you to have wisdom and insight you otherwise would not have but you need.

The severity of the needs of your parent determines where you should start in looking for assistance for her. In cases such as my parents where they only need some light help, such as doing laundry and housework, but not around the clock medical care, the library is a great place to start. Libraries may seem outdated to many people, but they are still chock full of information about every imaginable subject. My local library carries information at the front of the building about all kinds of local services and organizations, including many whose focus is the elderly population. I found a booklet at my library full of the names of businesses and organizations that help seniors as well as their contact information. Check your local libraries, as they may have similar useful information. Ask someone at the information desk for help if you are unable to find anything helpful. That is their job, after all, to find helpful information.

If your parent needs more in depth assistance, check with your local Department of Aging. They can offer you some great advice. They also can have a case worker from the Department of Social Services meet with your parent to assess her needs, then find home health care aides and other assistance. Many people qualify to have free or low cost assistance. Even if your parent is financially comfortable, this is often a good option, because the Department of Aging is a wealth of resources. They can direct you or your parent to most if not all of the help that she needs.

Local churches also may offer assistance. Many have programs to help people in the community whether or not the recipient is a member of the church.

There are things you can get around your parent's home that may help them too. For example, medical help devices are a great idea. They are devices worn around the neck or on the wrist, and if your parent has a medical emergency, she simply presses the button on the device. An ambulance will be sent to the home immediately. Many of these devices have a sensor inside that detects if the wearer falls, so even if your parent would be rendered unable to press the button, an ambulance still would be dispatched to her home in case of emergency. Some work only in the home, but there are also types that work anywhere, I believe using cellular technology.

GPS and tracking devices are also a good option, especially if your parent has Alzheimer's disease or dementia. Wandering is a very common behavior of Alzheimer's patients, especially as they are in the higher stages of the disease, and this can be very dangerous for that patient. Tracking devices can be worn or put on a key chain and carried with the patient at all times. If the patient disappears, a person with the tracking device's app on their cell phone or computer can find out where the patient is quickly and bring that person home.

Many wrist worn tracking devices also have a cell phone feature. Some are extremely simple and those appear to be the best for dementia and Alzheimer's patients. Some have the ability to store up to five phone numbers. The wearer pushes the button, and the first number on the list is called. If there is no answer or voicemail picks up, it goes automatically to the next number on the list and so on. Also, the device has a speaker so the wearer can speak easily with the person on the other end. Personally I think this is a fantastic idea!

If your parent has Alzheimer's or dementia, find your local chapter of an Alzheimer's organization. There are many Alzheimer's organizations out there with many locations, and certainly there is one near you in your state. These organizations are an incredible wealth of resources! They can provide tons of good information about not only what to expect as the disease progresses, but also caregiver information and support, where to find local assistance and even assisted living and nursing home information. Some even have support groups for caregivers and provide activities for patients and their caregivers such as a monthly luncheon. A quick internet search for "Alzheimer's organization in (your state or town)" will produce many, many results.

If your parent has a disease other than Alzheimer's, look around online. There may be organizations specializing in information and assistance for those who have the disease your parent has.

If you are like many adult children of narcissists, and are not in any form of relationship with your parent, then even you have one option that you can do to help your parent if you believe it is the right thing for you to do. Your local Adult Protective Services can help. Many narcissists end up completely alone by the time they reach old age simply because they have pushed everyone away with their terrible behavior. This is a dangerous place for them to be in, yet they do not realize that or the fact that they put themselves in this place. If you know your parent is in this position, you can contact Adult Protective Services. They are a part of Social Services, Department of Human

Services, Children and Family Services, or your local Department of Family and Protective Services. Different states use different names for the same organization. They will check on your parent's well being and intervene if necessary. This can be done anonymously. Even if you are unsure if your parent is being abused or neglected, if you have any doubts, it is often best to contact them to be certain the person in question is alright.

Chapter Eight – Filial Piety And Narcissistic Parents

I only recently heard the term "filial piety" for the first time. An online friend of mine taught me about it. She is of Asian decent, and said that filial piety is a huge part of her culture.

From what I understand, filial piety comes from Confucianism, and is taught to school children starting very early. It is the belief that children are to respect and obey their parents no matter what, and the children must repay their parents for raising them by taking care of them when they become elderly and frail. Some areas like Taiwan have laws in support of filial piety. Filial piety is said to be the greatest virtue one can achieve. In fact, the belief runs so deeply that there are negative words in Chinese and Taiwanese specifically to describe the adult child who does not perform their filial duties.

Many older folks in cultures that support filial piety move in with their adult children, whether or not they are ill. In families with more than one child, it is the home of the "chosen" child that they move into.

Due to filial piety, many older people have no sense of boundaries. They think it gives them the right to do and say whatever they like, and their adult child must tolerate it. If their adult child is single, especially if the child is female, she is expected to abide by filial piety, and basically sacrifice her life to care for her parents.

Not to go along with filial piety can mean you are an "unfilial son or daughter." Parents will claim this adult child is a bad son or daughter and wicked. The adult child's reputation is greatly tarnished. Friends and family may abandon him or her.

There is good news. Filial piety is starting to become less common, thanks to younger people who realize its flaws. It is, sadly, still very common with more traditional families who live by Confucian philosophy though.

It seems to me that this mindset can help promote and encourage narcissistic behavior. It can give narcissistic parents free reign to abuse their child under the guise of filial piety.

Unfortunately for many people subjected to this philosophy, it means that no matter what, they must have some sort of relationship with their narcissistic parents. In this case, prayer is your absolute best place to start. You will need wisdom on how to handle this relationship, and God certainly will provide it for you.

I also recommend seriously limiting your contact with your narcissistic parents as much as possible. This way you are not "abandoning" them, merely limiting your time together.

Answer their calls only when you feel able. For me, I pray when I see my parents' phone number show up on my phone. If I feel God is saying do not answer, I do not answer. If I feel I am able to answer, I do so.

Also, offer no excuses why you have not taken their calls. It is not their business what you do with your life. You are an adult, and you pay for your phone, so no one, including your parents, has the right to demand reasons why you did not answer their calls.

When you must spend time with your parents, remember, they are narcissists. You are not the problem, your parents are. You are not what they say you are either. You are a good person. **Not tolerating abuse does not make you a bad person.** You are still a good person, just one with healthier boundaries who has realized you have the right to protect yourself from their abuse.

Limit the time you spend with them. You have the right to say you are only spending two hours with them instead of six, for example. Stick to your schedule, too, otherwise they will see you as having weak boundaries and run roughshod over all of your boundaries.

Have and enforce good boundaries. Be fully aware of what you will and will not tolerate from your parents. If you are unsure of ways to enforce your boundaries, ask God. He will give you creative and effective ideas.

The more you focus on getting healthy and having good boundaries, chances are, the more your parents will pull away from you. Filial piety does not change that narcissistic behavior.

Chapter Nine – Stories About Caring For Narcissistic Parents

When I began this book, I thought I would include my own story about caring for my narcissistic grandmother. Instead, after some thought and prayer on this topic, I decided to interject some of my own experiences here and there where appropriate rather than tell the entire long, drawn out and depressing story. It is neither a nice story to read or for me to tell, so I opted to leave out much of it.

Instead, I thought it would be a good idea to share stories as told to me by other caregivers of narcissistic parents. These kind and lovely ladies graciously allowed me to share their experiences with you. I am not using their real names in order to protect their privacy.

By reading their stories, I hope to help you to see some of what worked and what did not work for them, as well as what their narcissistic parents did to their caregivers/adult children while they were caring for these people. Different perspectives and solutions can be extremely helpful sometimes, especially when we are talking about dealing with narcissists. As surprisingly similar as many narcissists are, they often react differently to similar circumstances. Hopefully, when you read this book and in particular these stories, you will have a better understanding of what it can be like to care for your elderly narcissistic parent.

My goal with this chapter is to help prepare you as much as possible to be your parent's caregiver if you opt to do so, and reading about others' experiences may help you in that area.

Rose's story...

"As a caregiver for my dad, I found that I had to be the parent. The older he got the more he depended me, like a child. I had to be tough at times, which I wasn't use to, especially with him. After all, he was dad.

He had OCD (Obsessive Compulsive Disorder), and his obsession changed every month or so. That wasn't easy to deal with, because he was so demanding.

He was never diagnosed as a narcissist, but he had many of the traits. He sure didn't show any concern for my well being. He always came first, and he wasn't very honest. Lying to me came easy for him. It was as though I wasn't real to him. I was only good for what I could do for him.

During the year and five months I cared for my dad, I had no life. I took care of him alone, and being recently divorced left me with no help. It was very hard on me due to all I had been through with my dysfunctional family. My narcissistic mother had recently passed away, which left Dad empty. He gave up on life. He just didn't know how to live without her ruling his daily living. But, he was my dad, and I did love him. More importantly, I love God.

Maybe being an empath or a scapegoat had influenced me to take him in, but I don't regret my decision. He past away last June and I do miss him. Funny thing though: I don't miss my mother."

Angela's story…

"When I was a child my mother often threatened to send me to live in a children's home. My father left just after my seventh birthday. I had a brother fifteen months older who was the golden child and I was the scapegoat. My brother left home when he was eighteen.

The last few years I lived in my mother's house, she did her best to persuade me to move out. She charged me double the rent that anyone else I knew was paying their parents. I was considering how I might be able to manage to leave when my mother had an operation and complications afterwards. I stayed to look after her.

Soon after that, I got engaged and stayed to save to get married. I couldn't understand why she didn't like my man, or why the arrangements for the wedding caused so many arguments. It didn't occur to me at the time that she might be jealous and doing her best to sabotage my happiness.

My mother paid for driving lessons for my brother. When I reached driving age a year later, my mother refused to pay for any lessons for me, so when I started work, I paid for lessons for myself. It took me awhile to learn to drive. We never had a family car, because my mother couldn't drive. I had no idea about driving, and my coordination is poor. After I passed my driving test, my mother bought an old car and started to learn to drive.

At the time, I wasn't happy in my job, which my mother had applied for on my behalf while I was away. The only decent thing I had to wear to the interview was a pale, insipid looking dress, and my mother refused to help me purchase a new one.

After I started work, I bought myself a new dress designed to be worn over a sweater or shirt. My mother angrily told me that short sleeves should not be worn over long sleeves, and this annoyed her for a few weeks. Then one day, she proudly appeared in the same dress in a different color!

She finally agreed to let me apply for a job at the firm where she worked. Now I could drive her to work. When I had my mother in the car with me and we got to an intersection, she would lean forward and look from side to side to see if the road was clear. I couldn't see past her, and would get beeped at for not moving. I was still telling her to sit back and keep still years later.

After learning to drive but before she had passed her test, my mother decided she would drive to work with me sitting beside her. I explained I didn't think I was the right person to sit with her. I wasn't an experienced driver, I didn't think I could explain driving to anyone, and she didn't listen to a word I said anyway.

One icy morning, she insisted on driving. On a country road with a car coming in the opposite direction, my mother swerved the car, lost control, and we ended up slowing sliding into a ditch. We were unhurt, and someone stopped to help us. They gave us a ride. After that, whenever there was snow on the road my mother didn't drive, but when it looked like it might be icy or similar conditions to when we'd come off the road she still insisted on driving

After she passed her test, she wanted me to accompany her to visit relatives. To get there, we had to ride on the interstate. Not having a death wish, I refused. This was never forgotten, and I was blamed for her never becoming a highway driver.

When she became elderly and after a serious illness during which she hadn't been able to drive, my mother decided she wanted to start driving again. She asked me to sit beside her while she drove to a local shop. Against my better judgment, I finally agreed. She drove along with one hand weakly on the steering wheel and the other resting on her lap. I told her to put both hands on the wheel because she wasn't in full control of the car.

Mother wasn't happy about the way I'd spoken to her while she was driving, and took the car out on her own a few times afterwards. This was concerning to me. I felt she wasn't safe on the roads and her sense of direction, which had never been good, was now obviously much worse. She soon decided that she would no longer drive, because other drivers were beeping at her and she was getting scratches on the car. Thank the Lord, there was no loss of life and the scrapes had been made on a wall, not other vehicles.

And so it was then that I became her driver.

I don't enjoying driving. I know other people can happily drive along while holding a conservation, but I can't. I can manage a light conversation driving along the straight—aways, but questions where I have to think about the answer while I need to concentrate on driving is not something I can cope with. Here is where my mother found the chink in my armor.

I got angry with her, told her not to do it, and delivered a few hard truths from my heart and mind. Then she would get upset and say I should be able to do it by now. It was one of the things I found most frustrating about looking after her. It took me awhile to work out how to deal with this. She mostly seemed to start asking questions just as I really needed to concentrate. Ignoring her completely, I started to calmly talk myself through my driving. "I need to be careful here. There's somebody right behind me, and I'm coming up to an intersection. Turn on turn signal, slow down, and stop. It's busy, now it's clear and I can go." I'd gotten her keep quiet, even if it was just for few minutes.

Coming out of hospital after she been in for awhile, my mother could never contain her excitement, and was particularly annoying at these times. I'd given her a packet of tissues once while she was in hospital, and wasn't expecting them back. She went on about giving them back to me, and I wasn't responding. It was a busy road, and I was judging when I could move into the outside lane to turn at the intersection. The tissues were then waved in front of my face obscuring my vision. No harm done but I wasn't pleased.

I was taking her to do her food shopping one day. We'd recently had a visit from my niece/her granddaughter. My mother was saying how lovely Joanne was, and that she was a very attractive girl. She finished off by saying, "Laura's not very pretty, is she?" referring to my daughter. I said I thought that she was pretty, and left it there. In my mind, I looked at it objectively. Anyone looking at the two girls would probably find them equally attractive, and consider them both to have a pleasant personality. I, of course, consider my own daughter the prettiest. She also has a great sense of humor and a lovely nature. I considered my situation. I couldn't really stop the car and leave my frail elderly mother at the side of the road, so I felt I had better press on.

I've related this story to friends, and they've reassured me that my daughter is pretty. I told them, "That's not the point. I'm used to ignoring my mother's nasty remarks. It's that she did it when out of the kindness of my heart I was taking her to do her shopping."

Coming back from shopping one day, my mother tried to get me to agree with her that mothers preferred their sons and fathers preferred their daughters. (We bought our eldest child up as male but she is now living as a female. My mother never accepted this, and continued to call her by her original name.) She'd recently seen how well our youngest daughter and my husband got on. I replied that I loved both my children equally, and how much I loved seeing Laura and her father together. Then I said I liked the idea of fathers, but I didn't know what having one was like because I hadn't had one. That shut her up.

Here's some history behind my mother's remarks:

My mother told me that she was happiest when she was newly married and had my brother. When I arrived only fifteen months later, she didn't want my brother to feel left out. My father was in the navy, and my mother was staying at her mother's house while my father was away. My mother looked after my brother, and my grandmother looked after me. When I visited one of my aunts with my husband once, my aunt told him that I was hers (not literally) because she'd also looked after me when I was small.

As I grew up, my mother was constantly singing my brother's praises to other people. She told me once that she couldn't remember me growing up.

In her later years, she wrote a letter to an old friend telling her what I was doing for her. Her friend wrote back and reminded her that she'd tried to get rid of me while she was pregnant.

My mother always claimed that she was never ill, and as I was growing up she did enjoy good health. From the age of seventy—two however, she had one health problem after another. She'd get over one thing, be OK for a while, and then something else would happen. She would suddenly become very ill and need to go into hospital. This was how I ended up visiting her daily to check and she if she was OK, how she was managing, assessing her, and what her needs were.

When she was obviously very ill and couldn't even sit up let alone stand, she would tell doctors that she was OK and not in any pain. I then had to explain to the doctor how ill she really was. When she was well, she did her best to look after herself and wished to remain as independent as possible. At the same time, she seemed to regard me as her personal slave who she could call at any time to instantly do her bidding. I tried to manage her expectations as best I could. I felt I had to put my own life on hold, couldn't pay as much attention to my family as I wanted, and was living her life with her. It wasn't doing my own health and well—being any good, but I didn't feel I had any option. Requests for help to my brother and his wife were met with refusal to help.

I treated my mother with respect, doing things for her that she would never have done for me, while doing my best to ignore her narcissistic remarks and lack of respect for me and my feelings. All of the time I was with her, I wasn't being myself, I was hiding my feelings and being careful what I told her about myself.

My brother and his family moved away, and when my mother first became ill, we invited her into our home each week for Sunday dinner to get her eat a good meal. My mother would ask my children something, they would reply, and then my mother would start talking about how well their cousins were doing. She showed no interest in my children and asked no further questions. Eventually with my husband and children there, I challenged her about this. I also told her that she never showed me any sympathy when I was ill except when I had laryngitis. I felt fine, but had just lost my voice. Thinking about it now, if I wasn't talking to her, she wasn't getting her narcissistic supply. Likewise when I had a blocked inner ear and couldn't hear her, because she kept talking to me on the wrong side. The doctor had told me to use a nasal spray and come back in a fortnight. Mother couldn't wait that long for it to work, and kept telling me to go back.

My brother was the golden child, and I was the scapegoat. This continued with my brother's children and mine.

My daughter Laura and her cousin Matthew are the same age. They took exams at the same time. Matthew, at a different school, got his grades first. My mother came around and said to Laura, "Matthew's got all As and Bs, did you?" We explained Laura hadn't yet had her grades. When Grandma returned to find out, Laura had already decided that she wasn't going to tell her and told her so. She'd worked hard, done well but her grades weren't quite as glowing as her cousin's. My mother came to me to find out. I told her that Laura didn't want her to know. "Yes," she said, "but you can tell me." "I'm not going to betray my daughter's trust." I replied. Laura carried on studying hard and now has a really good job. All of my mother's grandchildren are lovely people.

Both of my daughters were kind to their grandmother and did their best to engage her in friendly conversation. Behind their backs however, my mother would say to me, "Laura doesn't like me," and, "Simon can do what he likes, as long as he doesn't do it around here."

When my mother became elderly, she asked if she could come live with me and my family. There was no way I was going to live in the same house as her ever again, and no way was she going to upset my family and destroy our life. She was very fortunate that a new block of apartments for the elderly was being built close to where she lived. After seeing one of the lovely apartments specially designed for older people, and with some persuasion, she agreed move. Mother then told everyone, in my presence, that I was abandoning her and putting her in a nursing home. The fact was she was going into her own apartment where she would still be as independent as possible, and I could carry on doing all the things for her that had been doing. She would also have a wearable call button, a button in the bedroom, and a cord in the bathroom to call for help in an emergency. She also could phone the staff to ask for help with anything she needed.

When my mother moved, she continued to call me for trivial things that she wanted done immediately, which could easily have been dealt with by the staff or even her neighbors. However, when she was ill and really needed my help, she would tell the staff not to call me. I never understood why she did that or why she told doctors she was fine and not in any pain when it was obvious to me that she was seriously ill.

My French class, one morning a week, had become my only me time. I went one morning with a headache hoping it would clear but it got worse and worse. When we took a break, I told the tutor I would have to go home. I rang my mother and told her what had happened, and said that I was going to bed. I thought I'd managed to make sure I wouldn't be disturbed. I had just gone to sleep when my mother called. It took me a while to work out what was going on, where I was and why. She was talking away about trivial things, and I struggled to understand what she was saying. After I hung up the phone, my head was still thumping, and I really didn't feel any better. I tried to get back to sleep but couldn't. I rang my mother and yelled into the phone, "This has got to stop!" I then told her she'd woken me up. "Oh," she said weakly, "Are you feeling any better?" This was one of the few times I got angry with her. I'd learned not to show my emotions. It did, however, seem to have some effect.

When I realized that my mother couldn't remember what I'd told her I was doing at a particular time, I bought her a pretty diary with lots of room in it to write my appointments and activities in it as well as hers, although I hated having to let her know what I was up to. (If you decide to do this, it doesn't have to be entirely truthful and you don't have to put everything in it.) I had been going round to check she was OK after my appointments only to have her say, "Where were you? I kept ringing you and you weren't there." At first, if she read that I had an appointment at a particular time, she'd still be ringing me right up to that time and immediately afterwards. I had to explain to her that she had to allow time for me to get there and back.

When we bought phones that could be programmed to give callers their own ringtone, I chose a cheerful, humorous one for her. Previously, I used to tense up every time the phone rang and I had to answer it because I didn't know who it was, if it was important or not. We also got caller ID. Sometimes I would get numerous trivial phone calls from her within a short space of time. With her own ringtone I knew immediately if it was her and could decide whether to answer it or not. If I'd already spoken to her, I didn't answer if I was getting ready to go out or I could hear the phone ringing before I'd even got back into the house. If I'd just got home, I could relax and ignore her until I was ready to speak to her. I also knew the voicemail would record any important messages.

Looking after a relative with dementia is extremely challenging. That being said, I feel that looking after an elderly narcissist with dementia can bring extra challenges. All their worst traits become magnified, and they think they can say whatever they like without any regard for the feelings of others. It was difficult to know what parts of my mother's behavior were due to her dementia or whether she was just behaving badly.

When one of my mother's sisters developed dementia, my mother showed a distinct lack of understanding, and was very disparaging about her. My mother declared that she was much more

81

intelligent than her sister, and that she herself would not suffer from it. As soon as she heard that her sister had died, she insensitively called one of her sons to see if she could have some of her sister's furniture. They didn't give it to her.

It became obvious to me, seeing so much of my mother, that she had dementia long before I could convince other people. When I explained to my brother what had been going on, he just said, "Well, she seems alright." Even the medical profession didn't diagnose her immediately. She did a very good job of covering it up. When she was diagnosed, she was in complete denial that she had it. If doctors mentioned it, she was quick to inform them that she was an intelligent woman, and had held down a good job. There's nothing wrong in doing your best, and I'm sure it held her good stead.

My mother would get important medical phone calls. When I arrived to see her, she would tell me that someone had called, but she didn't know who or why. I was left guessing as to who I should contact to find out what we needed to know. I wrote a letter to her doctor explaining that it would save us all time and effort if they contacted me directly. After asking my mother if this was OK, the doctor agreed. There was one time this didn't work. The doctor had decided she needed an urgent scan, and went back to her office to arrange it. After awhile I wondered why I hadn't heard anything about it. The doctor came to see my mother, and was concerned that the scan hadn't been done. She went away and rang the hospital. A nurse had rung my mother directly. My mother had told her that she was alright now, and that she didn't need it. She ended up having an operation, which I wasn't sure about putting her through, but it went well. On we went, thinking we'd been round all the hospital departments apart from maternity until something else would happen and we'd end up at another one.

My mother became very impatient. She didn't like having to wait in a hospital. When she was going to have a scan, if she was an out-patient, she thought she should go before people who were already in the hospital. If she was an in-patient, she thought she should be given precedence over out-patients. She never seemed to give any consideration to other patients and the fact that they needed treating too.

Despite having dementia my mother was able to dress herself correctly. She hadn't bothered to prepare meals from scratch for years, and preferred the quickness of putting a ready made meal in the microwave. If she couldn't remember where the bathroom was, she only had to stand up and take a few steps and she could see where to go. When she was well, she could manage quite well in her own little apartment (with me helping every day where needed), and I knew she was in a safe environment. There was only one time she got up in the night and left her flat. A member of staff found her waiting in reception to go to her lunch club. Her doctor was the person who'd managed to persuade her to go the club. When the doctor saw Mother again and asked her if she was enjoying it, she told her that she hadn't wanted to go before, because she thought they were a rough lot. She actually met up with a dear neighbor from where she used to live, and ladies she had met at the school gates when we first moved to the town.

My mother embarrassed me several times in the hospital with the things she said in the hearing distance of others, even before she was diagnosed with dementia. I could only hope they didn't think I felt the same way.

My mother looked at a young black girl sat close to us in a waiting room and asked, "Do you think there are a lot more black people around now?" Not really what you want to have to put up with when you're not well and waiting to see a doctor. I'm not always quick to think of a good reply, but I wished a few days later that I'd have thought to say, "Isn't it wonderful how God has made us all different."

In a room full of people waiting for minor operations, there was a nurse calling people and then telling them where to go. I'm always grateful for nurses doing the job they do. Mother, however, decided to say how fat she was, and how she ought to take more care of herself.

We were waiting in a waiting room full of people where we always seemed to have to wait a long time to see a charming and well respected doctor. Mother said, "Perhaps he's having sex." I responded with, "Would you like to look at a magazine?" She said, "Yes, I'll have a look at The Country Life." People have found this story really funny and hopefully no one took her seriously, but it's not done to tarnish a good doctor's reputation, is it?

My husband and I went to see my mother after she'd had an operation. The lady in the bed opposite had been friendly towards her. My mother said, "These people have some very unattractive visitors. I thought her daughter would be pretty." She was pretty. The only ugly things in the room were mother's heart and mind. I said, "Perhaps they don't like the look of you either."

It was funny watching her do her best to get out of hospital after a stay. As soon as she went in, she would be asking when she could go home. She'd start getting herself dressed as soon as she could. Then she would start preparing for the questions she knew the doctors would ask her. She would ask us, "Can you get me a paper so I know what date it is? Who's the president?" I suppose she didn't like the indignity of being in hospital.

I could never understand why my mother liked charming, smarmy men. They gave me the creeps. I thought she was a bad judge of character, but she must have enjoyed the attention. She really liked white male doctors, and she could be inappropriately flirtatious. She would pay a lot of attention to what they were saying and was more likely to do what they advised. Once a young Asian looking doctor arrived to assess her the morning after she'd been admitted to hospital. My mother started talking to him as if he'd just got off the boat. He crossly told her where he'd been born and had grown up. "Oh, that's close to where my mother's family came from." I said, "We often used to go there to visit them." If the doctor happened to be female and looked foreign, my mother really didn't pay them much attention at all, and it was obvious she thought they didn't know what they were doing.

My mother found being old and frail difficult to bear. She said, "I never thought I'd get like this." The first time she told me she wanted to die, I didn't know what to say.

She had always been a regular church attendee, but now that she was old, that changed. She decided that she no longer believed in God, and that she wasn't going to heaven because of what she'd done. What she thought she had done, she didn't say. She still, however, enjoyed going to services at her residence. Also, once a month on a Sunday afternoon, I would take her to a short service at my church for older people living alone, followed by sandwiches and homemade cakes. So whenever she said she wanted to die, I would appeal to her past belief, and tell her that if she was called she could go, but if she wasn't, I'd carry on looking after her.

When I was a child, my mother told me that when someone died in our family, a relative who had already died would come to get them. When my mother was ill, she often said she'd dreamt about her father who she'd been close to. One day when I saw her, she seemed to be asking me to finish her off. "No way," I thought. "You've caused me enough trouble. I'm not going ruin the rest of my life for you." I said, "If your father comes to get you, you can go." I then added, "If my father comes to get you, don't go." He'd left her to raise my brother and me on her own. He had died about twenty years before.

The following day, when I went to see her she said, "I dreamed about your father last night. He told me to buck myself up, and pull myself together!"

PS. I've just realized, my father was sixty—one when he died, and the same age as I am now. I am determined to enjoy my life now in my own quiet way. Life is too short to worry about a lot of the things I worried about before."

Chapter Ten – What To Expect When A Narcissistic Parent Dies

While at the time of me writing this, both of my parents are still alive, I got a glimpse into what it is like to lose a narcissistic parent when my narcissistic maternal grandmother passed away in early 2002.

My grandmother stopped speaking to me in early 2001 for reasons unknown. She got sick at some point during that year and ended up in a nursing home for her final few months. I never went to see her, and she did not ask to see me, as far as I know. No one asked me to visit her or said she wanted to see me, so I assume she did not want to see me. The day of her viewing then funeral, I went to the funeral home before the viewing was to start to say my good byes. I figured she would not want me at her funeral, but I felt I needed to say good bye. This seemed like a good compromise. Once it was done, I began to grieve and it was the most complicated grief I have experienced.

Mostly, I grieved the fact that my grandmother and I did not have a good relationship. With as much time as we spent together during 2000, you would think we would have grown close. We did not, and in fact I realized just how much she disliked, even hated, me.

It hurt me very much, so I naturally was very sad about it. I also felt guilty for not being whatever it was she wanted in a granddaughter while at the same time, being angry that she made me feel that way. The worst was I was relieved she was gone, and I knew that I never had to deal with her again. I felt absolutely horrible that I could be glad my own grandmother was dead.

As time passed, I began to see that my feelings were very normal under the circumstances. Of course I did not grieve her in a normal way, like I did when my paternal grandmother died. My grandmother on my father's side was a good, loving, kind lady, so losing her hurt a great deal. Losing the grandmother who ordered me around like I was the hired help, trash talked me behind my back and maliciously attacked me as well as anything that I cared about meant that losing her felt absolutely nothing like losing my other, much kinder grandmother.

I have met many adult children of narcissistic parents who had experienced the death of a parent, and shared their stories with me. It turned out that our stories were quite similar. I thought that it was actually uncanny how many of their stories were quite similar to my own.

Grieving the death of a narcissist is a hundred times more complex than normal grief is. Normal grief has several steps. Some people say five, others say seven. I tend to believe there are seven steps in a normal grief process…

1. **Shock or denial.** The inability to accept that the person has passed away. This phase may be as brief as a few moments, or it may last as long as a few weeks. It varies from person to person.
2. **Pain and possibly guilt.** The pain of living without your loved one starts to sink in. It feels

unbearable. You also may feel guilt over things you did or did not do.

3. **Anger and possibly bargaining.** Anger that the person has been taken sets in. If the person did something that caused his death (driving recklessly, for example), you may be especially angry at your deceased loved one for quite a while for causing his or her own death. You also may try to bargain with God to bring that person back. "I'll go to church every Sunday if you just bring him back!"

4. **Depression.** The pain of your loss hits you hard. You may isolate yourself. You think about things you did together or wanted to do together. This is totally normal and do not let others, no matter how well meaning, make you feel like there is something wrong with you at this stage. It will end, but only if you feel it instead of stifling your emotions.

5. **Moving on.** The depression starts to lift.

6. **Working through things.** You are able to think more clearly than you have since losing your loved one. You start to look for practical ways to live without your loved one.

7. **Acceptance.** You accept the reality of your situation. You may not be happy but you are less depressed. You realize you are a different person now than when your loved one was alive, and you accept that about yourself.

These steps certainly are not written in stone, of course, but they are often basically how most people experience grief after losing someone they love. They also usually happen in this order, although sometimes a person may bounce back and forth between a couple of steps for a while, most commonly anger and depression.

When a narcissist dies however, these steps are very different. I believe it is more along these lines:

1. **Shock.** Anytime someone dies, even after a long illness, there is some degree of shock involved. Like in a more normal grief process, this is when it is hard to accept the person has passed on. It may last a few moments or a few weeks.

2. **Acceptance.** You accept that the person has passed away.

3. **Relief.** You suddenly realize that you are free from the drama, the abuse, and being used. It feels good, but this feeling does not last long at first.

4. **Guilt.** You feel guilty for being relieved that person is gone. You beat yourself up for being so cruel. How could anyone be glad their mother (or father or grandparent or whoever) is dead, you ask yourself. You think you must be a horrible person.

5. **Depression.** You get sad because your relationship with the narcissist was such a waste in so many ways. You are sad that you did not have a good relationship, a typical parent/child relationship. You are sad for the time you lost tolerating the abuse.

6. **Anger.** You get angry at the narcissist for being so cruel. You get angry about the fact your

relationship was terrible when there was no good reason for it to be that way. You remember painful things that you had forgotten about or deliberately had not thought about, and they make you angry. You are angry for tolerating the things you did, for not realizing just how bad they were for so long.

7. **Acceptance.** You start to accept the facts that this person was extremely abusive, and you are normal for feeling the way that you do.

8. **Moving on.** You begin to enjoy your new found freedom. Thinking about that person still makes you sad and probably always will to some degree, but it is no longer devastating.

These steps may not happen in this exact order. In fact, I found with myself, I bounced back and forth between most of them quite a few times, as have other people I have spoken with who lost a narcissistic parent or relative.

There are also plenty of people who upon losing a narcissistic parent do not grieve per se. They simply feel relief that person is gone and they are now free from the abuse and oppression their narcissistic parent provided. To many people, this sounds completely heartless. Obviously, these people have not grown up with a narcissistic parent! Even if you do not feel the same way, you certainly can understand how someone could when you think about the circumstances.

After the initial grieving, sometimes people experience more or intense emotions. A very common experience is a great deal of anger to surface. Memories pop into the forefront of one's mind about some of the awful experiences, which can make anyone angry. It feels like it happens completely out of the blue, but the fact is when you stuff your emotions down inside, as most children of narcissists learn early in life to do, those emotions will come out at a later time. They simply mean these are areas where you need healing. Just because an abusive person died does not mean you are suddenly healed and whole. Healing still needs to take place.

In addition to anger, you may feel an incredible sadness and grief. Not because you miss your narcissistic parent, but because you never had the parent you wanted and now the possibility of that is gone. No doubt you knew while your parent was alive that she was incapable of being the good, loving parent you always wanted and needed. Yet even so, once that parent dies, the chance of her changing is gone forever, and it really hurts. You may grieve for what never will be. The finality that death brings can dredge up many painful feelings about this topic.

Some people may feel nothing when their abusive parent dies. Sometimes things were so horrific that any positive feelings for the abusive parent died in their child well before the parent died. Sometimes when the adult child has ended their relationship with their parent and the parent dies years later, they feel nothing. The parent feels more like a stranger than a parent, so it is no wonder they feel nothing.

In many cases, the adult child of a narcissistic parent feels a lot of guilt when the parent dies. Whether it is because they felt relief, felt nothing or felt regrets for not trying harder (even knowing nothing they did would be good enough), that guilt can be very painful.

Some people were blessed with witnessing change in their narcissistic parent before her death. Granted, it is very rare, but it is possible. They suffer so much when the parent dies, because they finally got to have a good relationship with their narcissistic parent, then she died before they were done enjoying it.

One thing that may help you to cope with your emotions is to write your parent a letter. No one but you has to read the contents of the letter, so you can feel safe to let it all out however works best for you. Getting things out will help you to feel so much better, even if it is simply in a letter. You can say all of the things you wanted to say to your parent when she was alive, but you know she would not have listened to or would have used to hurt you with somehow.

I did this when my narcissistic grandmother died. I wrote her a letter, getting all of my frustrations, anger and hurt out at her. I then placed it under her headstone. It was very healing for me.

I also talked to God a lot during that time. I really did not have anyone close to me that I felt I could be totally honest with about my struggles anyway, and He is always the best one to go to in my opinion. He helped me to look at the situation objectively, which gave me a much better perspective on it than I had previously. I realized that although my grandmother disliked me that did not mean I was a bad granddaughter. I was good to her in spite of how cruel she could be. Her stopping speaking to me in her final year was also not my fault. She never even gave me a chance to find out what I did that she found so wrong. How could I try to fix things when I had no idea what the problem was? I also remembered some things my mother had told me about my grandmother. My mother did not have an easy life, being raised by my grandmother. That does not give her a free pass to be abusive, of course, but the fact is, she did not deal with any of her issues. How could someone who did not face anything be anything but dysfunctional? God used my grandmother's death to help me start to forgive my mother.

On top of your complicated and painful emotions, you also will need to decide whether or not to attend the viewing and funeral services if they are to be held. Relatives and friends of your narcissistic parent may not like you attending, especially if you have gone no contact, and you may end up on the receiving end of their wrath. The likelihood of this increases if you have not been in contact with your parent for some time or if your parent has told others how "mean" you have been to her. Is going worth putting up with such behaviors to you? If so, go, and stand proud. Anyone who would act up on such an occasion truly has no class. Their opinions should mean nothing to you.

If you do not think you can handle going, you might want to do as I did when my grandmother died. Visit the funeral home prior to the viewing. In my experience, most people who work in the industry understand that families have problems. When I went to the funeral home that morning of my narcissistic grandmother's viewing, the staff could not have been kinder or more understanding with me. They allowed me a while alone with my grandmother to say goodbye. One man even hugged me as I cried.

Or, you could visit your parent's grave once the services are over. This way, you can avoid all potential contact with others, and say your goodbyes in private.

Losing a parent is a very painful challenge in life. When the parent is a narcissist, there will be more complex emotions. You will get through it though. It will be hard, and it will change you, but you will survive, and even thrive.

Epilogue

Unfortunately every situation with narcissistic parents is unique, so there are no easy, one size fits all answers. Even so, I hope this book has been a blessing to you. I am praying for every person who reads this book.

Please remember to keep God first in your life, and talk to Him often about your situation often. He will provide you with the answers you seek. Lean on Him to give you strength and courage too. He will!

If you are still in a relationship with your narcissistic parent, especially if you are in a caregiver role, please also always remember to take care of yourself. Whatever helps you to keep your peace and remain sane and grounded, do it. Self care is vital, but perhaps no more vital than when in a relationship with a narcissist. You are of no good to anyone, especially yourself, if you are physically and mentally under the weather. Taking care of yourself should be your absolute top priority after your relationship with God.

Also be certain to nurture relationships you have with supportive, healthy, loving people. People who you can confide in without fear of judgment. People who will love you and gently tell you the truth, no matter what. These people are true gems, and you need them! Do not neglect them even if you are busy. Make time and an effort to spend with them.

Do not neglect blessing people. It feels good to do nice things for those you love or even complete strangers. Both the giver and the receiver are blessed.

My prayer for you, Dear Reader is that God may grant you whatever you need to enable you to handle your relationship with your narcissistic parents with grace, love, kindness, strength and courage. And, may He bless you richly in every area of your life.

With Love,
Cynthia

Index

About The Author

Cynthia Bailey-Rug is happily married to Eric Rug. Together they live outside Annapolis, Maryland with their menagerie of lovely pets.

Cynthia has been a Christian since 1996, and believes God has called her to write. She always loved writing, but realized it was her purpose in 2003. She has since written many articles and books. She also has edited books for other up and coming authors. She enjoys reading, animals, classic cars, crafts, gardening, electronic gadgets, and spending time with her friends, family and pets.

Where To Find Cynthia Bailey-Rug Online

Website: www.CynthiaBaileyRug.com

Facebook: https://www.facebook.com/TheButterflyProjectMD/

Facebook fan group:
https://www.facebook.com/groups/FansOfCynthiaBaileyRug/

Twitter: https://twitter.com/CynthiaRug

Blog: https://cynthiabaileyrug.wordpress.com/

Linkedin: https://www.linkedin.com/in/cynthiabaileyrug

Tumblr: http://www.tumblr.com/blog/cynthiabaileyrug

Google+: https://plus.google.com/+CynthiaBaileyRug

Amazon: http://amazon.com/author/cynthiabaileyrug

Smashwords:
https://www.smashwords.com/profile/view/CynthiaBaileyRug

Made in the USA
San Bernardino, CA
28 December 2018